Every Thing Has a Spiritual Solution

Stories of Awakening, Transformation and Healing

Bob Switzer

Every Illness Has a Spiritual Solution,

Stories of Awakening, Transformation and Healing

Copyright © 2013 Bob Switzer

All rights reserved. No portions of this book may be reproduced or transmitted in any form or by any means, electronic or mechanical, including photocopying, recording, scanning, email, or any information storage or retrieval system.

Printed by CreateSpace, North Charleston, SC

Library of Congress Cataloguing-in-Publication Data

Switzer, Bob

Every Illness Has a Spiritual Solution, Stories of Awakening, Transformation and Healing

Library of Congress Control Number: 2013920044

ISBN 13: 978-1492287520

ISBN 10: 1492287520

Spirituality, Personal growth, Alternative and Natural Health and Healing

Disclaimer Statement

The suggestions given in this book are to help the reader make their own better, more conscious choices about behavior, lifestyle, modalities and professional medical support that suits their unique needs. Not all of the information, statements, advice, opinions, or suggestions contained in this book have been evaluated by the FDA or other health review authorities in other jurisdictions, and therefore should not be relied upon to diagnose, treat, cure, or prevent any condition, disease, illness or injury. This book is for informational purposes only. The author of this book does not provide medical advice or prescribe the use of any techniques for physical, emotional, mental or medical problems. The publisher and author do not make any claim as to the accuracy or appropriateness of any course of action described.

The intent of the author is to only offer information of a general nature to help the reader in their quest for good health. In the event you use any of the information in this book for yourself, the author and the publisher assume no responsibility or liability for the use of any information or material in this book, or your actions or outcomes.

The Author and publisher are not affiliated with, do not endorse, and assume no responsibility for any individuals, entities or groups who claim to be manufacturing or marketing products or services referred to in this book, or who otherwise claim to be acting in accordance with any of the information or philosophies set forth herein.

The names of the storytellers have been changed for privacy and these contributors have signed a release giving the author and publisher permission to use their stories in this book.

This book is a reflection of the author's own spiritual understandings and is not intended to speak for any spiritual path, teacher, or religion.

Other Soul Perspective Series Books by Bob Switzer

Thriving with Spiritual Intelligence

How to Adapt Yourself, Your Business or Professional Practice to Our Changing World

The Messenger of Machu Picchu

A Spiritual Adventure

Dedication

To all Souls

who want to go beyond

current apparent limitations

and into spiritual freedom.

Acknowledgements

I am in awe of the storytellers that Spirit connected me to for this book. Recording their journeys has been an inspiration and an awakening for me too, bringing the messages in this book into practical application. They have bravely endured pain and other challenges, have grown from them, made changes in their lives – transforming their lives physically, emotionally mentally and spiritually in their healing discovery processes. Thank you dear brave ones for helping the readers of this book by sharing the intimate details of your spiritual healing journeys.

Thank you Andrea as you read at our breakfast table each day, sharing your health findings with me.

Thank you Penny, Ingrid, Celia, Kathleen and Richard for your thoughts and encouragement early on in the writing of this book.

Table of Contents

Introduction

Part I	**The Soul Perspective on Illness**
1	Spiritual Principles of Life, Health and Healing
2	Your Destiny is Your Spiritual Blueprint
3	The True Purpose of Illness, Injury or Disease
Part II	**Purifying Our World of Passions, Poisons and Perceptions**
4	Latent Poisons in Your Environment
5	Our Passion for Harmful Foods
6	The Spiritual Gift of Accidents
Part III	**Cleaning Out Disharmonies in Our Spiritual Bodies**
7	Roadmap to Your Spiritual Bodies
8	Emotional Toxins
9	Uncovering Past Karma to Heal the Present
10	Do Your Thoughts Pollute or Purify Your Body?
Part IV	**Solving Puzzles: Uncovering Root Causes**
11	Tapping the Creative Power of Soul
12	Healing Metaphors: Solving Riddles of Illness, Injury & Disease
13	Finding Your Personal Path
14	Every Illness Has a Spiritual Solution
Appendix	Spiritual Qualities for Health and Harmony

Introduction

Our present state of health is a reflection of our unique make-up that has been formed over many lifetimes as Soul, our true identity, who we are at our core.

The Art of Spiritual Healing

In this book I examine the possibilities that we have within us the ability to change outcomes. It can mean making significant changes in your life, and so in reading this book I invite you to leave the logical mind behind and enter into a new space of oneness, connection and harmony with your higher self, Soul.

I have written this book as a guide to assist you in seeing the spiritual purpose of your particular illness and to work with the many spiritual tools that are provided in these pages to help you find a solution to your challenge. There is a spiritual answer for every health issue. However, we need to find our own path to wellness because we have created our current conditions in some way. And so our health and healing must also reflect the unique nature of our personal journey.

Taking action on your part regarding your illness or disease and creating your own path to healing is inherent in the process. Although the focus of this book is to help you uncover root causes of illness or injury, the same principles and processes can help you heal from other human situations such as poverty, addiction, injustice, and even a broken heart.

> *The process of spiritual healing teaches us something about ourselves we didn't know before. ….the approach assumes responsibility for whatever is wrong. Once we're willing to shoulder the blame for our thoughts and actions, the inner forces can begin to heal us, even as our understanding of the causes becomes known to us through our dreams or other means.*
>
> Harold Klemp, Author of Spiritual Wisdom on Health and Healing

Healing is a Personal Journey

We are fortunate today to have at our disposal a vast spectrum of modalities, information at our fingertips on the Internet, healing practitioners, drugs, herbal medicines, natural medicines, in fact an immense range of possibilities that can assist us on our road to healing. But which way to go? That is the key. Your way will be unique for you just as you got to this point in your life in your own individual way. And it will be your personal realizations and most important, the changes you make that will heal you in a true way.

This book is therefore also about helping you select your own personal path, which by the way may change as you go along it. One path may lead to a fork in the road, or a switchback, or a unique ride into the unknown. So one must be open, flexible and courageous to follow one's own route. But in the end, your direction will lead to harmony and balance because you have created it. I'm talking here about creating your own health and healing and *creating* is the operative word.

A true healing involves creativity, accessing the power of Soul, your true essence as a spark of the Creator. Creativity is going beyond conventional beliefs, attitudes, behaviours and current limits inherent in our make-up. This is the key to the process. But how to do this? It takes a willingness to heal, to stay well, and to work with your inner guidance.

Roger Faces His Challenges

I have known Roger for a number of years and admired his ability to do what he wanted to do in spite of his serious physical challenges.

He told me he first noticed that something was wrong in 1974. At that time his right eye suddenly went blind and he was diagnosed as having an inflamed optical nerve. He continued on with life normally in spite of his blind and lazy eye. In 1992, he developed a condition in his left hand that started with tingling and progressed to a lack of sensation. It was at that time his doctor did a round of tests and Roger was diagnosed as having Multiple Sclerosis.

Roger told me that at first he felt annoyed, even angry, but he remembered and heeded the doctor's advice not to identify himself with the disease. Roger told me, "It was my body, not the inner me that had the problem, and I carried on as normal." Over the next few years Roger's back became weaker, and it became aggravated after sitting and getting up off his chair.

One day in 1999 he woke up and was so sick, his whole digestive/intestinal system was in turmoil. He was very weak and he went to sleep at one o'clock in the afternoon and upon waking he could not lift his head. He was so incapacitated he had to crawl to the washroom. At the time, he did not associate the attack with M.S. Following this episode, the next day he was able to walk again, but his back got weaker and his balance deteriorated. He moved from the use of a cane to a walker in the course of just a few months.

As his health declined, he was resisting, he told me, denying that he had a problem, and then it dawned on him that these new symptoms were manifestations of M.S.! He had finally put the pieces together.

Taking Action

Three months later Roger began to research his disease on the Internet, investigating the symptoms. He started to check alternative ways to treat it using natural methods and by talking to many other people. It was at this time he asked Spirit, "How can I best help myself?" Roger was really starting to take charge, research his condition and to take responsibility for his healing as he opened himself to new opportunities. At first he found all sorts of what he described as "concoctions" and different products, and he started to consume large amounts of water, as well as receiving Reflexology treatments. Then a friend recommended a man for him to see, an energy and herb healer. This man gave Roger several different herbs, but the most important thing he taught Roger was that he was responsible for his condition and to "take responsibility for it." He realized that at some point in the past *he had set up the conditions for his experience today.*

It was at this time that Roger learned "this is a true blessing." He told me, "It allows me to see this as a chance to grow – Spirit is teaching me and allowing me to accelerate my spiritual growth." He added, "This is an interesting path I've chosen for myself." Roger had a profound personal realization; he recognized he had, at his highest level, chosen his M.S. experience for his spiritual growth!

Examining His Innermost Being

Today Roger is focusing on healing with many different products, foods and supplements and his progress has been steadily improving. He has been getting stronger and his back is more flexible. Roger described how he works with contemplative exercises and is learning to create "different forms of mental patterns." He is changing his thoughts and beliefs as he examines his innermost being.

This spiritual exploration has taught Roger how to rely on his inner being and his inner connection with God, whom he says has helped him significantly. He described it as "working together." As a result, he's getting better. Roger has now recovered the vision in his eye and he confided that had he not taken action he would have been wheelchair bound two years ago. He now walks with only the aid of walking stick, resorting to a walker only for long distances.

Acceptance has played a large part in Roger's healing. "I was an island, separate from Spirit and I now know that I am a part of Spirit and I am able to accept help from others. My most important learning is to be one with Spirit. Negative emotions separate you from Spirit."

New Goals and a Mission

Roger's goal changes from time to time but at the moment it's "to get well with a heightened sense of perception and spiritual awareness." Today he describes his mission as "helping others and really listening to what they're saying without judgment." He feels that working on stubbornness is a key theme related to his M.S.

I asked Roger if he could offer any advice to others with difficult challenges. He suggested, "Have a strong desire to get better. Take responsibility, and focus." Roger has taken even more responsibility by making a complete career transition from health practitioner to investment consultant (much of his work is via the Internet) in order to maintain his ability to sustain himself.

Roger's key is to look within for solutions.

Disease is a Lack of Harmony

Wellness is balance and harmony. Disease or being ill-at-ease is a lack of harmony in the body. Somehow, a part is out of sync with the rest and in order to heal, we must discover the cause of the imbalance in order to restore harmony and create a sustainable healing. Illness can be considered a gift, a spiritual gift to help one move forward in their life.

In chapter one I present several key spiritual principles that are important for your understanding in taking charge and applying creativity to your healing process. You may have doctors, medicines, and assistance and advice of all kinds, but the process, the pathway you take is in your hands. You are responsible for your own spiritual growth and healing, which really means a return to harmony in your being. Nobody can do this for you. This growth is a learning process, a process of discovery about yourself from a spiritual perspective. It is how Soul has chosen to learn at this point in your life. So in order to begin this voyage of discovery, you need to know the basic rules, some foundation spiritual tenets that are in operation in your life. So chapter one is key to your understanding as to how key Spiritual Principles affect the healing processes.

Spiritual Healing, a Changed Consciousness

In the chapters that follow, I move into how to use these Spiritual Principles in your journey of discovery. The entire process is about change. Something has to change in your life. You've heard the expression, "If you keep on doing what you're doing, you will keep on getting what you're getting." Something has to adjust and when you make a shift, or get an aha moment, the light of realization dawns on you and you solve a piece of the puzzle. You see, Soul wants to grow and the illness or condition has manifested to move you forward, to help you become unstuck, to let go and make the changes you need to live a happier life filled with joy. So this is a process of exploration of the hidden aspects of yourself - then making modifications. It's about wiping the mud off the mirror of Soul. Some changes are very difficult indeed, however in some way and in some fashion, if Soul wants change it will happen sooner or later. The more we are able to face change - often life-altering or life-threatening (as we see them), the quicker we will bring our body back into harmony.

At its simplest, a true healing is a changed consciousness. It comes about through a modification in beliefs and in faith. In the process you have purified a little or a lot, and in effect you have moved closer to God. That is, you have become more God-like in your character and in the way you approach life and your interactions with others, nature – in fact all life. (Please see a list of God-like/spiritual qualities in the appendix at the back of this book.) In the process then, Illness serves to move Soul forward on Its journey of purification, becoming a greater vehicle of love.

As you become more aware of your true inner identity and gain a deeper understanding of the meaning of life, it becomes easier to see that all of life is about growth. We are here to learn and so the challenges of life are lessons to teach us about living from the highest perspective in harmony with the whole. To do this one cannot be the victim of circumstances nor blame anyone or anything for troubles or challenges. All the solutions to our challenges are within our capability to solve.

About the Stories of Healing Journeys

A key theme I've highlighted in the telling of all of the spiritually transformative experiences that form part of this book include a willingness on the part of the person to take responsibility for their condition and search out a solution. As well, all storytellers I interviewed use contemplation regularly to tap the creative power of Soul. Many also use sound in combination with contemplation, chanting HU, Om or other spiritually charged sounds to help them connect with their inner realities. The discipline of all of the storytellers, to varying degrees, in recording their dreams, realizations, spiritual experiences and in writing down their healing progress, physically, emotionally, mentally and spiritually are also common factors of success in making life changes and resolving their healing crisis.

I believe we each discover and hold our own truths, mainly because we are unfolding at our own pace and in our own way. What follows in this book are my truths about spirituality as applies to healing. Yet there are many paths to truth and you will need to find your own truth to authentically heal well. If something I say does not resonate with you, please take what fits well for you and leave the rest. I believe there will still be value here for you within these pages.

So I invite you to read on if you are ready to take action on your part and discover new things about yourself that could help you find a new balance and harmony in your life, healing aspects of your being in the process. Following the self-directed processes I outline in this book will help you discover the spiritual purpose of your illness, injury or disease, uncovering root causes in the process, and point the way to resolution of your condition.

> ***Everyone has his own specific vocation or mission in life; everyone must carry out a concrete assignment that demands fulfillment. Therein he cannot be replaced, nor can his life be repeated, thus, everyone's task is unique as his specific opportunity to implement it.***
> Viktor E. Frankl, Author of Man's Search for Happiness

Part I

The Soul Perspective on Illness

Illness serves to move Soul forward on Its journey of purification, becoming a greater vehicle of love.

1

Spiritual Principles of Life, Health and Healing

High ethics and religious principles form the basis for success and happiness in every area of life.

John Templeton, Mutual Fund Pioneer

Timothy's Transformation

Timothy shared with me his experience losing his wife to Cancer and his journey into spiritual healing. I'll let him tell his story in his own words:

...During the last days of Ruth's life she was mostly asleep. Blood loss from the tumor lowered her blood pressure and she made it very clear she wanted nothing that would extend her life, as it was. Eventually the loss of blood left her in more of a coma-like state than just sleep.

On her last day she was very restless. I held her hand and spoke to her, hoping/believing that she could hear me. She remained very restless and seemingly agitated. I started to sing HU. HU is a chant, sung for centuries in many cultures around the world which brings the love of the Holy Spirit to those who are immersed in the sound. It is a love song to God and also an ancient name of God. As I started to sing Ruth noticeably started to become calm. I sang on for many minutes and she was peaceful. Within minutes of my stopping her agitation returned. I sat with her and sang again. Again she became peaceful. This was repeated many times and it was obvious that the HU song was bringing about this calm and peaceful response.

I have a CD with about four thousand voices singing HU for about 20 minutes. I started to play this CD and the same calmness came over her. I put it on a repeat play and let it go for many hours at a low volume. She stayed in that beautiful state until the end. I had checked her at about 9:00 pm and she was still with me. At 9:15 she was gone.

I was so happy that I was able to realize what to do to make her last hours in this physical body, peaceful, calm and surrounded by the sound of LOVE.

Daily Contemplations Bring Healing

Now Timothy had to live with the loss of Ruth. His daily contemplations kept him in tune, to keep his heart open to Spirit. Timothy continues, "During that time after her passing, I felt like I was in a constant contemplation/spiritual exercise all day. I had grief but my spiritual attunement helped me to move on almost immediately. Keeping the spiritual reality in mind helped me through the loss process. I realized it's how you deal with it, not what happens to you that counts. Once one has the awareness that death is not final, it really helps."

Timothy felt if he could get a sign that she was OK, he would feel a lot better. One day Timothy saw that his picture of nine spiritual masters had fallen to the floor off a counter. He picked it up, asking himself how it could have fallen. There was nothing that could have moved the picture. "Could this be my sign?" he asked himself. Not being certain, he asked for another sign that she was fine. Later on he found the picture on the floor again. Now he knew she was OK!

Timothy feels that the time after Ruth's passing was a time of tremendous spiritual growth for him in detaching from the material stuff of life. "I'm in a totally different place than where I was. Before

I was concerned about material things, money etc. I have let this all go. None of it matters anymore," he shared. "What does matter is love – caring, allowing others to be who they are. I feel a level of respect for others as Soul. It feels to me like I am more accepting and less judgemental of the behaviors of others."

Detaching from Anger and Fear

Timothy also feels like he has let go of a lot of anger, what he called "righteous indignation." And certain fears have been let go of as well, particularly in the area of finances. "Now I can be concerned, without being fearful," he confessed. And this has also affected his feelings about himself. "I'm being myself now. I can be more authentic. I can do what I want in the face of other's opinions. I feel I now have the ability to say 'no' without feeling bad about it because as Soul, I know I'm responsible for everything I do. I need to have integrity for myself. As a result, I'm getting more in touch with who I really am."

On reflecting about his fears in financial matters, Timothy also shared with me something interesting about healing. He said, "When I heal an aspect of my life, I've discovered that the healing process passes on to my children." Timothy gave me an example. He told me about a financial issue that his dad experienced, that he was dealing with and also that his son was having too. His dad has now passed on but that still left Timothy and his son with the "heritage issue." Timothy had taken the issue into contemplation on numerous occasions and reached a point one day, as he describes, "I knew the issue was gone. The next day my son called to tell me that his issue was gone too. From that day forward my son's business took off."

Karma and Purification

Timothy also commented about the pain Ruth suffered at the end which he feels was karma. "It really hurt me to see what she went through." But he now feels his understanding of karma has expanded. "We all need to work off karma," he said. "Some translate easily, others have pain. We need to see it as purification."

Timothy told me about another thought he had about his spiritual consciousness. "Since Ruth translated I have had two out-of-body experiences (vivid and real spiritual experiences) of significance. Both were inner initiations. I don't want to go into specific details but in general in both cases I was at a Wisdom Temple in the inner worlds and undergoing a spiritual test. I was unaware that I was being tested, however. In both cases I failed the test, at first, but I learned from the experience. I was tested again and, in both cases, my spiritual guide came to me and told me I had passed the test and was ready to move on to the next level. This was quite clearly an inner initiation, a spiritual acknowledgment and feeling of consciousness development. I was very grateful for the experiences as I felt I was growing spiritually."

Timothy has been able to move into a new relationship and continue his life journey with a new partner.

Spiritual Giants and Key Principles of Life

I chose Timothy's experience to share with you in opening this chapter on spiritual principles because there are so many of them illuminated. The rest of this chapter will highlight some of these keys to understanding life, health and healing.

As in all jurisdictions, it is important to know the laws in order to operate at maximum efficiency. The Spiritual Principles that follow are no different. I've included just a few in simplified form to give you a spiritual grounding and to help you understand that you are constantly evolving, which implies change to bring your life into harmony with Soul and your spiritual destiny.

There is a body of wisdom and truth at the root of all great teachings and philosophies; the heart of all that has been brought forth by the

Avatars of these great teachings is love. These spiritual giants include Buddha, Jesus, Muhammad, Zoroaster, Krishna, Rebazar Tarz and many others who were carriers of the Light of God. They were enlightened souls who chose to teach of the spiritual nature of humankind.

Wisdom Comes From Within

They taught that wisdom comes from within. It is not of the mind and is therefore much different than knowledge. Wisdom is a function of inner experiences, realizations of truth we each can experience for ourselves in our own way and in our own time. Everyone's experience will be different when the exploration begins in earnest.

Spiritual healing involves making more conscious choices in concert with your true self (Soul), allowing one to see more clearly what one needs to do to heal. Life becomes smoother as you follow your inner guidance with an understanding of the seven universal principles or laws that follow.

You have to leave the city of your comfort and go into the wilderness of your intuition. What you'll discover will be wonderful. What you'll discover is yourself.

Alan Alda, Actor, Director, Screenwriter and Author

Principle 1
Soul
Your True Identity

You are a spiritual being called Soul having a human lifetime.

You have been given a physical body to wear.

You also have an emotional body, a causal (karmic) body and a mental body.

You don't have a soul. You are Soul.

You have a body.

C.S. Lewis, Author and Poet

Principle 2

Spiritual Growth

Why You Are Here

You are enrolled in a schoolhouse called Earth.

You have agreed to learn some lessons unique to you, so you have consented to grow in many ways.

Your lesson plan is your destiny.

As you are totally unique, as is everyone else, you should not judge the lessons, struggles or the approach to lesson challenges others employ.

Neither should you judge yourself by what others can do, need to do or achieve.

Growth is the only evidence of life.

John Henry Newman, 1801 – 1890
Evangelical Oxford Academic

Principle 3

Karma

Motor for the Wheels of Change

Your past thoughts, words and deeds have resulted in your intellect, character, talents, genetic (health) predispositions and life lessons today.

You are attracted to people and places due to your need to work out karma (karmic attractions), creating opportunities for growth and purification.

Changes result from your need to learn and grow in different settings such as family, other relationships, health conditions and work, and from your reactions to these life situations.

Change-growth is a process of trial and error. There are "miss-takes" like in the film-making process until you get a "take", until you get it right.

In this process, you create your future which is determined by how you interact with others today. What you think and what you believe forms your future.

Debts that must be paid ... that sums up the concept of karma. But I would add that karma is not a burden that you have to carry. It is also an opportunity to learn, a chance to practice love and forgiveness, a chance to learn lessons that are valuable to us. Karma offers us the chance to wipe our dirty slate clean, to erase the wrong doings of the past.

J.P. Vaswani, acclaimed thinker and philosopher

Principle 4

Detachment

Accepting Change Gracefully

You have a collection of props for your settings in each stage of life including people, possessions, career, financial resources and health.

To move forward through your lesson plan you will need to learn to let go.

This letting go includes emotions, thought patterns, beliefs, attitudes, possessions and people, which no longer serve your lesson plan for growth.

The ability to readily detach from these things that hold you back makes for a much smoother, healthier life.

Detachment is also having the patience to wait for the right moment for Spirit to make a connection for you – i.e. surrender, letting go as an individual so that God can guide your life.

Every possession and every happiness is but lent by chance for an uncertain time, and may therefore be demanded back the next hour.

Arthur Schopenhauer, German Philosopher, 1788-1860

Principle 5

Harmony

Moving to the Rhythm of Life

Being human, you will likely resist some changes that are part of your lesson plan.

Your resistance may cause disharmonies within your being comprised of physical, emotional, causal (karmic) and mental bodies. This can lead to disease.

Disharmonies resulting in "dis-ease" may also come about via genetic influences which carry lessons you need to learn.

When these lessons are realized and actualized, your true Being is realized, and harmony and abundance is restored.

Going with the flow (of life) is living in harmony.

Health is a state of complete harmony of the body, mind and spirit.

When one is free from physical disabilities and mental distractions,

the gates of the soul open.

B.K.S. Iyengar, founder of Iyengar Yoga

Principle 6
Creativity
Tapping Soul's All-knowingness

What you make out of life is up to you. You have free will.

You have been given all the skills, talents and tools you need to solve your challenges.

Creativity is a key tool and includes going within through contemplation, meditation, prayer and quiet time.

Imagination, visualization, asking for help, listening and being open to answers in whatever form they come, are an important part of the creative discovery process.

Creativity comes from looking for the unexpected and stepping outside your own experience.

Masaru Ibuka, co-founder of Sony

Principle 7

Love

It is All

There is an overarching agenda; Soul wants to grow, to expand in consciousness.

Service to all life is Its goal and eventually becomes Its mission.

Love takes on new meanings in this, a process of awakening.

You learn to give love to all by selflessly serving all life without thought of return.

At this point you embody many spiritual qualities that are aspects of love, but chiefly humility, forgiveness and compassion.

This unfoldment is a spiritual healing process.

Love is not a matter of belief. It is a matter of demonstration.

Therefore, if you desire love, try to realize that the only way to get love is by giving love. That the more you give, the more you get; and the only way in which you can give is to fill yourself with it, until you become a magnet of love.

Paul Twitchell, Author of Stranger by the River

On Spirit, Soul, Light and Sound

While we are discussing Spiritual principles, I feel it is important to provide some clarity around the terms *Spirit* and *Soul,* as I make frequent references to these in the coming pages.

What is Spirit?

Scientists in recent years have confirmed that there is a basic substance, or unit of energy at the foundation of everything in the universe that they reference as the Quantum Hologram. Others call it the Divine Matrix, the "energy" that forms the common denominator of all of creation. Mystics think of it as the Body of God.

Many call this energy, spiritual energy. I reference it as Spirit. Others call it Holy Spirit, Divine Spirit, the ECK, Prana, Chi, the Voice of God, the Life Force, or the Audible Life Steam. It sustains and is the basis of all life. This spiritual essence connects everyone with the heart of God or the Creator and it manifests and can be felt or experienced by human beings as spiritual sound and spiritual light in its two basic forms of vibration. These twin aspects of the universes of vibration can become guideposts for us on our spiritual journey back to the heart of the Creator – moving into greater purification and spiritual healing. When we have these uniquely personal experiences with spiritual sound and/or light, we know we are connecting to Spirit.

How does Soul relate to Spirit?

Soul is an individualized part of Spirit, a unique consciousness, a distinct unit of awareness – who we really are.

Spiritual Principles, Secret Keys of Life

The spiritual principles presented in this chapter are just a few of the secret keys of life that have a direct bearing on health and healing. Keep them in mind as we begin to uncover the root causes of illness, injury, chronic conditions and disease in the chapters to come.

Our next step is to explore the destiny of Soul.

2

Your Destiny is Your Spiritual Blueprint

Love nothing but that which comes to you woven in the pattern of your destiny. For what could more aptly fit your needs?

Marcus Aurelius, Roman Emperor from 161–180 AD

Diane's Encounter with Destiny

When Diane was young she was told her knees would deteriorate and give her problems later in life. And so a couple of years ago when her knee stiffened and then became painful, she knew she would have to face this challenge and do something about it. It was bone on bone rubbing, and very painful. Diane recalled, "For two years I put it off. I felt I could fix it. During this time, I could feel the fears emerging inside me. I was thinking, what if things went wrong? What would happen if the surgery failed and I couldn't walk afterward? How could a failed operation be corrected?" Diane was gripped in this fearful consciousness and couldn't get above these emotions. "The negative was stronger than the positive at this time, yet I knew deep down that it would be very negative for me if I let this fear grip me for a long time.

"I finally went to see my doctor and then a specialist who told me I needed knee replacement surgery. It turned out I knew the specialist surgeon. We had connected many years before, so he was not a complete stranger to me. This was a comfort to me and calmed my fears down somewhat. I understood I had to have the surgery in spite of my doubts and worries. I knew then I could do this."

Listening, a Key to Acceptance

Diane continued, "In the process of acceptance of the reality of surgery, I had to learn to listen only to the positive and I had to learn to be quiet. I sang HU a lot, my way of connecting with God, and I also realized how powerful quietness is. When I had questions, I'd sing HU to tune inward or simply read a book title and then sit quietly, and I could feel my fear subside in the silence with no outside world buzz. The HU helped me open inner doors. This became my journey.

"A turning point for me in accepting the operation and moving beyond my fears was a dream I experienced. In the dream, my spiritual guide told me I was going to be OK. He said, 'Enjoy the journey.' I was sensing quietness and love at the same time, and it was a beautiful feeling."

"After my acceptance and surrender, everything I needed was coming to me in a natural way. I was open to messages. As a result, the rest was like a journey that was all arranged for me. One day I received an inspiration in my daily contemplation that I needed to work on my whole body before the operation; I needed to get much stronger and get in shape. When I came to that conclusion I was serendipitously connected with a personal trainer through a friend. I knew this is because I had surrendered to Spirit. The trainer had extensive experience working with people who were recovering from knee and hip replacement operations. And so I was able to exercise my core and knee before the operation, for knee surgery was major – it was a new body part like getting a new heart part. So part of accepting the surgery was accepting my new body part. I knew I'd have to like my new knee.

"I remember going into surgery singing HU. I had no memories after that and woke up with my new knee. I looked down at the bandage and said, 'I have a new friend. I was accepting it. At times I cried after the operation for no reason. On one occasion I asked, 'What have I done?' As I sobbed, a nurse heard me and spoke some words of understanding, validating my emotions over letting it all go. That helped me move on and I never cried again. I transitioned to accepting my new knee like a friend. I was walking again without pain." Diane likened the feeling by saying, "It's like getting a new heart. It's not yours. There is an acceptance needed."

Writing it All Down

Diane's journaling played a major role in her speedy recovery. "Writing in my journal, I could feel the love of the gift of a new knee. I discovered through my writing I had to learn how to receive, how to accept something that isn't mine. I questioned myself: 'Why did I get it? Why am I supposed to have it?' And the answer came: 'It's what I need now.' I realized I tend to fight the idea of being deserving - accepting. I'm a caregiver – I would help others. This time the role was reversed. I had to be accepting, not giving. I had to learn how to receive love, and in the process, how to love myself. I realized I needed this in order to give love."

Before the operation, one of my fears was stairs. I expressed this to the doctor and he assured me he would ensure post operative training for stairs. But I still went ahead and arranged all of my furniture on the main level of my home so I could have one-floor living and not have to use the stairs. When I got home after the operation, I looked at the stairs and went straight up! I actually was doing stairs better than walking. It was a mind thing. I had to move past the mind.

Today I'm more aware of what I eat. I'm aware of my weight and I'm more in tune with the vegan way of eating. I'm trying not to abuse my knee. It's making me more conscious of taking care of myself so I can take care of my knee.

Key Lessons on the Way

Diane learned many valuable lessons on her journey. "I learned how fear can creep into your life, like the fear of having to depend on others, but knowledge helped me overcome it. I'm more trusting now; the process taught me to trust and become quiet. Life is very, very peaceful for me.

"My nature is to find humor in things, but I lost it for a while when I was in fear. Having a strong spiritual focus in my life made life a little easier. It gave me a live-in-the-moment attitude, to just let it be.

"I've learned more about detachment – not to be so attached because these things can be taken away. I lost my knee, but got a new one. I say, accept what you get given back to you. It may not be the same thing – be thankful.

"I'm grateful for these medical gifts we have today. I now look at people and surroundings the same way, with gratefulness. My knee got me through another go around – I couldn't walk – I was given another so I can move on with my lesson plan, my life."

Diane knows now. "These things are written in your destiny," she counsels. "There is a reason. So accept. Live through it, then you are on the other side of it – and changed in the process. I find it's now easier to accept the bumps in the road and keep going. I say thank you for the experience. Learn to love. Roll with the punch – you can get through anything. Don't abuse what you are given.

Diane's final word: "Love what you are given. Love the gifts in life. I'll have two as I'm having my other knee done as well. Learn to accept and love whatever you are given. Everything is positive in life. My knee has healed so fast, it's like I never had a problem!

Destiny of Soul

A key spiritual principle presented in the first chapter is that you are an eternal spiritual being called Soul and are here in this earthly body having a human experience. And, like Diane, you have a destiny – a spiritual blueprint of sorts, a set of lessons and experiences that you agreed to as Soul. In other words, you accepted a form of contract to grow up and live within a set of circumstances that offer challenges from which you can learn and grow as Soul.

Our life as Soul having a human experience is like attending school, and each day we have the opportunity to learn more lessons in the way we interact with others and all life as we move through our spiritual curriculum. You may think the lessons including illness are too tough at times, but Soul has not chosen any challenge that is too great for it to deal with. All of life's challenges have a solution and provide invaluable learning.

Think back to a time when you were faced with a challenge. How did working with this challenge change you? Did you feel stronger, more confident or perhaps more resilient or flexible as a result? Did you grow in some way?

There's Always another Opportunity

Life is a series of challenges of some sort or another, some we fail and some we conquer. Therefore our growth comes out of a process of trial and error - but there are really no errors, just growth for Soul. So our life is a process of experiences from which we learn. There is no failure really, only missed opportunities for Soul's growth. There is always one more opportunity, as there is always one more step in the growth of Soul. Lessons are repeated until they are learned. In fact, lessons keep returning as we reach higher and higher levels of understanding of certain issues that Soul has chosen to focus on. Every part and action of life contains an experience for Soul's growth.

All the world's a stage, and all the men and women merely players: they have their exits and their entrances; and one man in his time plays many parts...

William Shakespeare, *As You Like It*

This Spiritual Blueprint, your destiny, can take you down many roads because you have free will, but all paths will yield the experiences and lessons you need to advance spiritually. There are times when we feel that our life is off-track, out-of-balance or in dis-ease, and it is possible at these times we have wandered too far away from our contract with Soul, or we have something that we need to learn that is now presenting itself as a test for Soul.

Making changes, redefining your life, is a part of this process of bringing your life back into harmony with your higher self, Soul.

We are the best we have ever been right now. In other words, we are the highest consciousness we have ever been in this present moment. This means that we are at the highest level of acceptance of our relationship with the Creator and at the highest level of accepting responsibility for our life.

Life is a process of becoming, a combination of states we have to go through. Where people fail is that they wish to elect a state and remain in it. This is a kind of death.

Anaïs Nin, American Author 1903 – 1977

The Journey is Paramount

As we begin to understand that life is more than a series of destinations, we begin to slow down and put as much attention on the journey. The process of getting to our endless destinations is as important as achieving the goals we create for ourselves throughout life. This realization is a major step in our awakening. It is the realization that, how we create our lives and the methods we use, are really how Soul grows, and therefore what is of ultimate importance. The journey is really what life is all about. The material goals like career, home, relationship and financial ambitions are simply tools for Soul's growth.

We have free will. What we do with our lives is totally up to us. We come into this world on our own and we depart on our own, and the only things we can take with us are our experiences. We have all the right tools and help that we need. We learn that life is about conscious choices and this is how we learn, from the choices we make.

The help we need for all of life's difficulties is right inside us. As Diane found, all the answers to all of our challenges are given to us if we ask. It is up to us to seek these answers and to use our creativity to draw them out. The process is a challenging one but rewarding for Soul. Knowing that all the answers are within, allows us to take a gentle approach to life. It allows us to walk in confidence knowing that all we have to do is listen for the inner nudges, or feel the heart to "hear" the call of Soul.

At some point, each Soul embodied in a physical body comes to realize that it is part of the "whole of life". And this "whole" is God. We are in essence like a molecule in the body of God. Like a drop of water is to the ocean, we are like the ocean...like the ocean in every respect but not the ocean. We are therefore all connected. When we change ourselves, we change the "whole", and so how we grow, interrelate, and live our lives influences every other being. Our thoughts, words and deeds are part of everyone's experience. We are all in this together, this schoolhouse called Earth (Shakespeare's stage).

As we live our lives, we are awakening to new levels of awareness of who we truly are and why we are here, and this is a never ending process of discovery and purification. As we grow, a part of us may become out-of-sync or out of harmony with our whole being, and this can manifest as disease, being ill-at-ease. In other words, growth causes change which calls for rebalancing – reharmonization. And vice versa; change can result in resistance which sets up disharmonies, possibly making us ill-at-ease as well. So we need to look in both directions - at what is changing and what needs to change.

> ***We are all in a process of transformation to something greater than our current state of enlightenment....and so it is a soul's destiny to search for truth in their experiences in order to gain wisdom.***
>
> Michael Newton, Ph.D.

There is always one more step in Soul's growth, in Its search for spiritual freedom. Chapter three delves into this more deeply.

3

The True Purpose of Illness, Injury or Disease

The truth is that our finest moments are most likely to occur when we are feeling deeply uncomfortable, unhappy, or unfulfilled. For it is only in such moments, propelled by our discomfort, that we are likely to step out of our ruts and start searching for different ways or truer answers.

M. Scott Peck, Psychiatrist and Author of The Road Less Travelled

Ian's Stroke of Insights

When I chatted with Ian, the twelfth anniversary of a life-changing event had just passed. The course of his life shifted dramatically the moment he had a stroke on the morning of September 11, 2000. He felt an intense pain in his temple, a pain he describes as ten times a migraine, then collapsed. He slipped into a coma which lasted for two weeks. He later found out he was in hospital without life support as he was not expected to live.

During this time Ian was present in the inner worlds (heavens), aware of being at a large ski chalet. He went outside, feeling as good as he has ever felt. Although it was night time in the inner worlds, it was much brighter there and the colours were much more intense. "I knew I was going somewhere else, so I just waited for someone to get me," he said. He remembers seeing Pierre Trudeau (the former Prime Minister of Canada) getting his papers together. Ian later learned that Trudeau had passed away during that time.

Ian came back to life on Earth and discovered he was partially blind in both eyes and was paralyzed down his right side, unable to walk. He quickly realized that there were a number of things he was not going to be able to do anymore such as driving, but he told me he also realized that he was "in good shape compared to many others in the world."

He spent the next year in rehab learning how to walk again. He also dealt with a mental fog, with the emotional shock of not being able to go back to work and the loss of friends at work. "I was in a state of confusion not knowing what I was going to do regarding income – my life."

Dreams Provided Acceptance

But Ian had been provided a look into his future which helped to give him a level of acceptance for his new life. Four years earlier he experienced two dreams which stayed with him. Ian describes them as "telling-forth dreams." In the first, he and his young son, watched as a news reporter talked about an earthquake in his city, Vancouver. He went outside to see the damage; his building was intact but everywhere else was destroyed. In the second dream the whole landscape was gone - destroyed. "I knew something was going to happen but I was not sure what, but about a year after the stroke I could see that the dreams were preparing me for my future. My son in the first dream represented the new me, young and vibrant. These dreams gave me a level of acceptance of what had happened."

Adopting a More Spiritual Life

Ian picked up his contemplation routine during his recovery and then increased contemplating to twice a day, singing HU to strengthen his connection with Spirit, and attending spiritual classes. Ian came to a realization during this time; he had wanted early retirement and now he had it. He was not happy about how he got it, but he got it! "Be careful what you wish for," he cautions others. But he muses; "Now I can focus my attention on my spiritual life without job worries."

Ian also knows that there is karma involved with his new life. While in rehab doing a lot of physiotherapy, Ian was asking in his contemplations how he could improve his condition. He asked to be taken to the Causal Plane to give him a better understanding of the causal seeds (past life influences) he was dealing with. Over the last few years he had become aware he had gone through a series of spiritual tests. Confirmation came on one occasion when he was in a dream standing in front of a panel of what seemed like judges. They were discussing him and reaching a decision on whether he passed.

"With my efforts in daily contemplation, my higher senses have picked up enormously. Now I pay attention to my intuition and Waking Dreams, signs from spirit in everyday life. I pay attention to random small thoughts to get myself in tune with the nudges Spirit provides."

Ian confided, "I am not overly concerned with my physical body. I'm more detached now. I know I can always take care of myself." What has been a big help for Ian in his spiritual progress are his dreams and the occasional out-of-body-experience. He records his spiritual experiences in his journal which make his spiritual life very real for him. "I've proved to myself life continues beyond death," he told me.

Today, Ian says he tries not to hold on to beliefs, "because there is a chasm between believing and knowing, and my spiritual exercises (contemplations) have helped me to move to knowing."

Ian admits the stroke has decided many things for him these days and changed him in many ways. He passes on junk food now and is living a moderate lifestyle. "Everything in the first part of my life is gone now – drinking, driving, television, work – I don't need them now. I have to live life with what I have created – my present paralysis and partial blindness. I feel like I'm purifying my being - like flushing a toilet."

Before, Ian's life was work, and that's all. Ian was focussed on what he wanted in life and gave those around him very little attention. His wife confesses that she was so detached when Ian was in a coma, she didn't care if he lived or died. Things are very different today. Ian now very much appreciates his wife who spent hours with him helping him to learn to walk all over again.

Realizations along the Way

Ian has come to major realizations about his spiritual growth; he is more aware of the need to unfold spiritually. "From this comes detachment," he told me, "and compassion." Today Ian devotes a great deal of his time to his spiritual growth with volunteer activities, spiritual classes, contemplations and more, and as a result he is more at peace with himself. In looking back at the last twelve years, he tells me his greatest areas of growth are: first, a heightened awareness and consciousness; second, being detached, not getting upset about a lot of things that used to bother him; third, living life with a lot less stress as a result; and last, a heightened level of creativity, tapping the creative power of soul.

His advice to others facing challenges is simple. He says, "Man be true to thyself. Be open to change and new information. Be resourceful and talk to others."

He added, as we finished our conversation, "I now know life down here is temporary."

Today, although Ian has physical limitations, he has gained something more precious; a new degree of spiritual freedom.

What is illness?

Illness or disease is a state of imbalance in the body. At its most fundamental level it is calling for change. To recap so far, we are Soul, a spiritual being having a human experience. This human lifetime is a stage that has been set for spiritual growth or purification. Soul has a lesson plan (a destiny); It has set purification goals for itself. It wants to learn new things, new behaviours, adopt new values, and most importantly move closer to being God-like. This means to be more spiritual-values focused in the way we interact with other and all life. (Please see the list of spiritual values in the appendix.) This is your path as Soul.

The movement to being more God-like embodies service to others. It implies less emphasis on the self and more on others. Spiritual masters, angels and guides are helping us in the inner worlds, and are completely dedicated to serving all life. This is our destiny as well, to become a spiritual master and serve all life. In the process we are learning, and this learning is affecting our core being in how we relate to all life.

Just like Ian, we are adopting new ways of being that can be described as taking on new qualities (of love) such as forgiveness, humility, charity, grace and dozens more.

So we are on a unique path, a personal lesson plan that is largely hidden from us. It's a mystery to be unravelled by following the heart, the gateway to Soul. Our goal on this path to true healing is to grow in some way or ways and this growth reflects in our consciousness, our state of being. Our consciousness is our acceptance of God in our life. That means, for example the degree to which we are able to accept change in our life. Expansion of consciousness involves exhibiting the qualities of God in our thoughts, actions and words. From a scientific point-of-view, try this on for size:

A human being is part of the whole called by us, universe, a part limited in time and space. We experience ourselves, our thoughts and feelings as something separate from the rest. A kind of optical delusion of consciousness. This delusion is a kind of prison for us, restricting us to our personal desires and to affection for a few persons nearest to us. Our task must be to free ourselves from the prison by widening our circle of compassion to embrace all living creatures and the whole of nature in its beauty. The true value of a human being is determined by the measure and the sense in which they have obtained liberation from the self.
— Albert Einstein

Our True Agenda - Growth

So we now have uncovered the overall agenda, our hidden mission, but we are not yet aware of the intricate details. However we have a starting point for understanding our imbalance, disharmony or disease. It centers on: first our lesson plan, second, becoming more God-like as a co-worker with all life, and third, changing consciousness in the process. It also implies gaining an understanding of Spiritual Principles or Laws so that we can live our life in harmony with them; inadvertently breaking spiritual laws can lead to ill health. Chief among them are the laws of karma, detachment and harmony (see chapter one).

As we grow in life, our lessons often present themselves as challenges and our responses to them. We typically learn best under pressure, enough pressure to cause change. These challenges can involve multiple lessons that are designed to purify us on several levels. After all we are a being, existent on several levels. We exist as physical beings but we also have other parts or bodies - an emotional body or component, a causal body (your karma that was established by your past thoughts, words and actions) and a mental body, the subject of chapter eight. All these aspects of our being must be in harmony, in synch. If one part is out of pattern, we are out of balance and there is the possibility that if we do not find the cause and correct it, we can fall into "dis-ease" in the physical body. Or this has already occurred.

A Healing is a Movement Back into Harmony

The healing process is one of moving back into harmony on all levels. It is therefore about discovery. One needs to see the bigger picture here. Much like the clothes you outgrew as a child, as your awareness expands, Soul becomes more active in guiding your life - you are more heart driven - but this comes with a kind of discomfort that arises from the realization that many of your scripts and beliefs no longer serve as they did before.

The discovery process is essential to unveiling the mystery of your disharmony. So an open mind is vital. We are dealing with aspects of you that have been a part of your physical, emotional, causal and mental make-up for a long time and are in totality what you are today. But this needs to change in some way for a healing to take place. A shift is being called for. Therefore, a realization of what needs to change is necessary. Perhaps by understanding the overall pattern of life we can unearth this treasure.

The Rhythm of Life

Our lives are ordered into cycles that follow life-wave patterns. These cycles are arranged into three, four, six and twelve year groups. The twelve year cycle is the most significant and starts with the year of our birth. The cycle of twelve also occurs in the months of the calendar, the signs of the zodiac, and in China, the twelve year animal cycle. Every prophet has twelve disciples. There are twelve basic mineral salts in homeopathic medicines, and twelve inches to a foot. All of human life is attuned to this number.

If we fall out of step with the rhythm of our life we can become ill, so understanding this twelve year cycle in your life can be helpful in seeing the overall pattern of Soul's journey, its educational lesson plan. Picture your life as moving in waves like radio waves, in three parts. Beginning the upward side of the cyclical wave you enter into a period of consolidation and purification (climbing upward). This is a time to go slower, to take your time, to review and sometimes go deep and take stock for the next phase. Sometimes these changes in your life can be very difficult and experienced at the top of the wave (years five and six) as a dark night of Soul. Here you can be passing through a period of change when your life is adjusting to new awakenings, new realities, purifying in many ways.

You then begin a new phase of the cycle on your journey on the downward (easier) part of the wave, the next six years of the twelve year cycle, having incorporated your new learning into your being. This can be expressed as a new feeling of liberation, a higher experience of choice and service in your life. When you reach the bottom of the wave you have reached a new level of spiritual fulfillment and consolidation, integrating changes into your way of being.

So we go through these three stages of the twelve year cycle repeatedly, needing to change what bothers us, a time of struggle looking for our new direction, possibly a dark night of Soul, and our eventual discovery of a new and better way to move forward in our life.

The Purification Process

As Ian's experience illustrates, a healing is a discovery about us that reveals something that needs to be purified, to be brought back into harmony with the whole or with Soul's destiny, its plan of growth. This is where the hard part can come in; it means that we are going to leave something behind that is no longer serving us well. This something could be a food, a drink, or an action on the physical. It could be an emotion that is no longer serving us like jealously or resentment. It could also be the discovery of a past cause that needs to be rebalanced such as a fear which is hidden in our make-up that is no longer serving us. It could be a thought pattern, a belief or value that is now worn out and is holding us back.

It also means that as we leave something behind, we bring something new into our life. This could be a new positive habit like more exercise in our physical realm. Or it could be by treating others with a more loving heart on the emotional level, adopting a new level of confidence in the face of a fear we are letting go of, or a new level of respect for others and their way of doing things on the mental level. It could also mean forgiving ourselves and others for what happened in the past in order to let that go as well.

So our goal is one of discovery to determine where the problems lie. They are usually hidden because we cannot see ourselves as clearly as other outside observers can see us. Others are usually better at assessing/reflecting/triggering our character than we are because we are looking at ourselves through the very old filters of our being that we are quite used to and take for granted. So these filters, these character traits, emotional responses and thought patterns and entire approaches to dealing with life are such a part of us that we can't see them clearly. It can take some courage and some discernment to open to a critical interplay with others and process the feedback, but you may find yourself opening up in this way in your journey of discovery.

Seeing the Cause of Stress

One realisation I came to a few years ago was that I was under stress. This stress was a result of too much work and it was now at a stage where it was throwing me off balance and I was seeing physical signs in my body like an upset stomach. In my process of discovery I uncovered a belief that my father had taught me and had served him well: Hard work equals success. So I had grown up believing that the harder I worked, the more successful I'd be. I've had to unlearn that belief pattern because I now know that for me, creativity equals success, and creativity is not fostered in a stressful environment. Creativity needs a relaxed state-of-being, and my very livelihood was being affected by my resistance to letting go of hard work and long hours.

So I had to unlearn this pattern and it wasn't easy. I felt guilty that I was no longer working hard when everyone else was. But my new creativity proved to me that I had made the right choice and my body also told me I had made the right transition. My stomach moved back into harmony (avoiding an ulcer) and life and "work" became much more enjoyable.

Taking Responsibility for Your Past, Your Present – Making Changes

So the process that follows is one of taking responsibility for discovering what needs to change within us. Together on this journey we are going to look into all of the dark corners and into the hidden reaches of our being to find the areas of purification that are necessary to create a complete healing and regain a state of harmony.

Let's start this discovery process with a look at our physical world.

> ***Every human being is the author of his own health or disease.***
> Swami Sivananda Saraswati, author of over 200 books on Yoga

Part II

Purifying Our World of Passions, Poisons and Perceptions

You are a one-of-a-kind being and your tests and challenges in life are also a custom package.

4

Latent Poisons in Your Environment

Clinical ecology (is) a new branch of medicine aimed at helping people made sick by a failure to adapt to facets of our modern culture, polluted environment. Adverse reactions to processed foods and their chemical contaminants, and to indoor and outdoor air pollution with petrochemicals, are becoming more and more widespread and so far these reactions are being misdiagnosed by mainstream medical practitioners and so are not treated effectively.

Richard Mackarness, MD – Clinical Ecologist

Bonnie's Purification

About 9 years ago, Bonnie began to feel more and more tired, like her adrenals were tapped. She told me, "When I was under stress it was more pronounced, and following some US Immigration procedures that required vaccination for Measles, Mumps and Rubella, as well as a TB test I noticed a significant decline in my health. My body was very tired and a lot weaker.

Bonnie's weakness persisted for several years, then things shifted for the worse. "About a year ago, I went through a period of high stress, studying late for several nights for an exam. At the same time, diarrhea started and got progressively worse, to the point where I was experiencing it around twelve times per day. My body was not absorbing anything and the added stress of starting a new job added to my toxic load. I lost twenty pounds in short order."

"I started doing research on-line for the possible causes of diarrhea and discovered the Specific Carbohydrate Diet. This is a diet high in carbohydrates that I began and it took the diarrhea down to about three times a day. Concurrently I'd been seeing my medical doctor who is also a Herbologist and she was busy ruling out all kinds of possible causes. She had heavy metals on her list of possibilities, but seemed to be looking in other areas. She recommended a colonoscopy, but the twelve hundred dollar ($1,200.00) cost made me pause to consider whether this was the right course of action.

"My husband and I had been doing muscle testing on my condition across a wide range of options and we came up with a positive on heavy metals, so on the next visit, my intuition was so strong that I was insistent with my doctor that I have a heavy metals test. The test results showed that I had off-the-charts poisoning for mercury and lead!

Bonnie told me, "My doctor started me on chelation therapy, however, the chelation pills gave me brain fog. I couldn't remember what I was doing and I'd put things where they didn't belong. I also had nausea and even threw up, and the diarrhea flared up again. I soon discovered that tests are only an indication of conditions, not conclusive. The chelation dosage was too much for my body and was making my predicament terrible, to the point that I was not functional - not able to work. In her notes about what helps, my medical doctor said that heavy metals collect in the bowels along with other places and that colonics were recommended as being very helpful. Well, I have been an enema pro for many years because my immune system has been less than robust, so as soon as

I started doing enemas, my diarrhea settled down. The only time I got it again was after chelation therapy, when the metals had been pulled out of all the places my body had stashed it, and they collected in my bowels.

Turning the Corner

"When I started chelation, my brother-in-law an intuitive/spiritual healer, heard about my condition and offered to assist me. I accepted and he took a look at my test results. In his treatments he began pulling the metals out of my body which made me very ill from trying to process the metals to eliminate them, but this was when I began to turn the corner. During one of his treatments, he said to me, 'Why is it that I love your body more than you do?' His statement jarred me. In that moment I realized that I didn't love my body!

"At the time, I was so drained that I'd abandoned my spiritual practices and physical exercise. I now realize how critical these are to good health and balance. I began to write in my journal about the issue that was surfacing about not loving my body and I came to the conclusion that I have never felt good enough. So I began writing fantastic things regarding myself and one day a message came through: *God thinks you're good enough!* I cried for five minutes when I had that realization. This was so huge for me that I made signs and put them up around the house.

"I had also started up again doing my daily spiritual practices, a visualization where I imagine white light vibrating every cell in my body and aura. As well, I had renewed my daily prayers where I ask for inner guidance and then I thank God for what I've received.

When I asked Bonnie about her level of involvement in her process of recovery, she replied, "All along I felt I'd been taking responsibility for my condition because I could see it was my karmic pattern: I knew I had to be very involved in the process which had led me to muscle testing and the help I received from my husband, brother-in-law and God.

Awakening to Self-limiting Beliefs

"When I turned the corner, it was really an awakening about self-limiting beliefs and it was my condition that helped me come to this realization – it was all the digging and soul-searching I was doing. My realization has helped me let go of the constant stress that was emanating from these deeply hidden feelings of not being good enough. In this journey, I've discovered that this feeling of a lack of self-worth was really a hidden fear, so I'm now better able to clearly identify what thoughts are mine as opposed to those that are negative.

"I'm now loving my body and knowing it is doing the very best it can given what I've put into it and the stresses I've created for it. And I'm loving it in spite of everything I had to go through."

Bonnie shared another realization she has had: "Loving yourself gives you greater love for others," she told me. "It helps you have a greater understanding and then caring for others.

"Today, I feel I'm more loving, but it's just starting. The metals dull a lot of feeling in the brain and as I eliminate them I am freer to have more emotional sensitivity and perception. My mantras are burning up old karma - old patterns - these days and my visualization powers and concentration are now better as I get rid of the metals in my body. I could be a completely different person at the end of this process! As I move into who I am and who I'm going to be, I know I have to be aware of the old me when it emerges, and let it go. So I'm keeping up with my spiritual practices. I need to slow my processes down so I can let go of old thoughts, behaviors and actions as they come up."

Bonnie has traced the source of her mercury poisoning to vaccinations and lead poisoning from living in close proximity to a major expressway and an airport for many years. She also told me about some aspects of her healing process that I am adding here in case readers find it helpful.

Other Notes from Bonnie

"I have found I have about two days of aftermath after I have finished the chelating pills and need to continue doing enemas. I've had to also make dietary changes as well because dairy and grains really affect my system adversely these days."

Being Conscious of Change

An obvious place for taking responsibility for your healing and well-being is in the physical environment. As you go through life, your body changes and so does your environmental setting. In all likelihood, what you could consume or tolerate in or on your body in your youth is going to change. This is a natural part of growing or aging. You need to accept this fact and know that you are going to have to make changes as you proceed if you want to stay in balance.

You are Unique

In addition, you need to appreciate that you are a unique being. What others can do or tolerate in and on their bodies may not be compatible with your body. You cannot judge yourself by what others can do. You have your own individual package of karma, genetic dispositions, emotions, sensitivities and preferences that attract you to certain environments, personal products, foods, work environments, residential settings etc. You are a one-of-a kind being and your tests and challenges in this life are also a custom package. These lessons are for your personal growth as Soul, so what works for everyone else may not suit you, and this includes what you eat, drink, work at, finances, and what you experience in your state of being. What is enjoyable to you may not be fun at all to somebody else. As such, your illnesses, your imbalances and disharmonies will also require a customized approach.

Key Questions to Ask

In examining your material world, this physical world, there are some key questions to ask yourself if you are dealing with a challenge that requires healing.

Has anything changed in your relationships, house, home life, work, entertainment, vehicle, financial life and hobbies? Changes in your life may have brought new intolerances or toxic substances into your sphere that were not present before. New subtle stresses may have lowered your immune system or your tolerance to certain things. These conditions may be temporary or represent new life conditions you need to work with, and include people, pets and where you spend your time.

Secondly, ask yourself, **Has nothing changed?** If your life appears static, a rare occurrence in my opinion, then perhaps something in your space has crept up on you and is causing a disharmony in your life. It could be your old house is getting mouldy and you haven't been down in the basement for a long time to notice. Or it's possible the orchard or farm you live near is spraying with a new herbicide or pesticide? Your street may now carry more traffic resulting in more exhaust or electromagnetic radiation (EMR) pollution. The high tension wires near your home may be carrying more current adding new levels of EMR's to your environment, weakening your immune system in the process. The same may be true of added electronics to your work or home environment like wireless devices. The key here is to think outside the box, look around, examine your life and your environment to see what could be at issue. Innocuous things should not be overlooked, as your unique constitution may be sensitive to something that you are not aware of at this stage in your life.

Purifying on All Levels

This lifetime is a voyage of discovery about ourselves and from Soul's perspective it is a purification process. As a reminder, we are not just purifying our physical bodies, we are purifying on all levels; our emotions, our Causal Body (Karmic Body) and our thoughts, attitudes, and beliefs carried in the Mental Body. (More detail on your higher bodies will follow in chapter seven.) So when one area is purified it is a little lighter. Its vibration has increased and so it calls for a similar shift in all of our bodies. As we lighten up on one level, it affects the other parts of us and when we do not make changes, we can eventually fall into a state of disharmony or "dis-ease" in that area. Growth is inherent in living, but the changes we are called upon to make in our life can be hidden. The mystery is before us, ready to be uncovered, but knowing where to look can be a challenge. But we do know that as we change, our outer world needs to change in some ways as well. So expect to make changes in order to move forward into a new state of harmony.

Bringing negative energies such as violence into one's life through exposure to certain movies, television programs, music, video games and reading material can have a toxic effect on our subtle bodies – our emotional and mental bodies in particular. The effects of these negative energies act as a pollutant on our being, so be conscious that every person, thing or experience we connect with either purifies or pollutes the body. This includes such influences as foul language, sexual references/behavior, anger/rage, greed or extreme materiality – all of these can exert a downward pull on our well-being, in effect dragging one into a lower consciousness or vibration, setting up disharmonies in the body. Even being exposed to extreme vanity in the form of arrogance or distain can have its effects.

Discovering Apparent Causes

Life can be a puzzle more often than not. What appears to be causing a problem may be a mask for something else. And other issues in life may not appear to have any physical causal origins. This is where you will need to begin to cast your vision in all directions and use some of the new exploratory tools I provide in this book.

Tobacco and Recreational Drugs: It goes without saying that these substances are obvious toxins and sooner or later will have a negative effect.

Allopathic Medicines: Most prescription or over-the-counter (OTC) drugs are known to have side effects which are really direct effects in your body. By taking a drug you are trading off the greater remediation power of the drug for the perceived lesser effects these can have on your body. So as stated before, be aware that what others can assimilate in their bodies may not be compatible with your body. I have found that the higher your awareness or consciousness, the more responsibility you have to take in solving your issues. Drugs typically mask issues. Natural remedies can also mask unless you are actively working with the process to discover what you need to change about yourself. Soul is calling for change, for growth.

A Lesson Hidden in Poison Ivy

While visiting Los Angeles and hiking in the Hollywood Hills, my knee brushed up against a Poison Ivy plant. Soon after, the Poison Ivy flared up, and later that day it started to expand alarmingly fast, looking like the start of a flesh eating disease. On arrival home two days later, my first reaction was to reverse a direction I had taken into natural medicine and I made an appointment with my old medical doctor. He prescribed a powerful drug. Within hours of taking the first pills, the Poison Ivy toxin in my body started breaking out at all of my joints – ankles, knees, shoulders, elbows, hips. I knew immediately I had done the wrong thing. I was trying to mask the message, what the illness was trying to teach me, what I needed to learn. My sister heard about my challenge and offered me a Reiki session which I accepted. While in the Reiki session, I went into a deep contemplation, and with the two combined, I received a flash of insight. I needed to take more control of my life in a certain area rather than just let it be. I was turning the issue over to Spirit and I should have been doing more about it. As soon as I got the message, I got a strong nudge to call my naturopathic doctor and he miraculously was able to see me the next day. He gave me a remedy and the Poison Ivy started to dry up immediately. Within two days there was hardly any sign of the issue.

The key for me was taking responsibility for the issue and being willing to uncover the message. At that point I discovered that Spirit was on my side in correcting the disharmony I had created, once I made a shift to taking greater control in the other area of my life.

Your Personal Environment

The areas where you spend your time are critical to your well-being. These include your dwelling, workspace, vehicle and where you spend time with entertainment, hobbies or sports. Have any of these changed recently? Today's buildings can contain materials for which you could have a sensitivity like paints, carpets, coatings on floors, air quality systems and more. Make a complete assessment of these areas for possible clues to sensitivities you may have. I recently visited a new model home for a housing development. The chemical odours were so bad I had to leave.

At work, do you handle glues, sprays, cleaners, toxins, fertilizers, herbicides, radiation, airport security scanners etc? Many of these modern products are deemed safe, but remember that you are unique. If you are reading this book, you are not typical. Any product can have an undesirable effect. *Don't judge your body by what others can do.*

The Pest Control Technician

I once purchased a fridge from a used appliance shop for a rental unit I owned. It wasn't long before the tenant called telling me there were cockroaches coming out of the fridge. I immediately called a pest control company. When I met the technician I was shocked at how disfigured he was. He had a large boil on his face, one eye was much larger than the other and he walked bent over with a slight limp. He advised me to clear the area as he put on a mask and began to spray the nest in the bottom of the fridge. In speaking to him after his spraying, it was clear that he did not associate his conditions with the chemical spray he was using!

The Larger Environment

Your greater environment includes many passive items that could be mildly or totally toxic to your system. These include noise, EMR's (electromagnetic radiation from high tension wires, electronic devices like computers and TVs) and solar radiation. Some feel we are all participating in a giant experiment in involuntary epidemiology — being irradiated by cell phones and towers, cordless phones, satellites, broadcast antennas, military and aviation radar, wireless mice and sound systems, internet, wireless LANs in schools and the workplace, energy saving fluorescent light bulbs and smart meters. And researchers know what it does to some of us. Two experts on these issues are Dr. Dietrich Klinghardt MD, PhD of the Sophia health Institute and the Klinghardt Academy, and Physicst and Microwave Weapons expert, Barrie Trower.

The main problem isn't Cancer as it takes a long time to develop. Other problems seem to show up first: neurological, reproductive, and cardiac issues. Also problems with memory loss, severe headaches, sleep disturbances, learning disabilities, attention deficit disorder, and infertility can show up long before Cancer. When Cancer does appear, it's typically brain tumors, leukemia, and lymphoma. So if you are experiencing any of these issues or symptoms, check your electronics environment. Any one of these influences could be compromising your immune system, or possibly the combination of effects is enough to cause your system to fall into "ill ease." Combine these influences with normal doses of stress and you have a compounded issue. So no one effect may be a cause; it may be a combination that is set off by a trigger like a change in your life that is causing anxiety or stress, or a change in diet.

EMR Precautions

The risks associated with cellular phones and other devices due to electromagnetic radiation (EMR) are emerging globally. Devra Davis, author of *Disconnect* and other experts suggest precautions you can take to avoid health issues including the following:

Use text features over voice calling and hold the device away from you;

If you must make a voice call, use speaker phone or a wired headset;

If you want to use a wireless headset, do it with a low-power Bluetooth emitter;

Do not carry a phone turned on next to your body;

Be cautious of radiation shields that claim to limit exposure to EMR's as they can reduce the connection quality, forcing the phone to transmit at a higher power output. The same applies to signal quality in your location. If low, (e.g. rural area or in an elevator) the weaker signal has to boost itself, increasing your exposure.

When it comes to other serious EMR sources, good alternatives are corded telephones, LED energy saving light bulbs, limiting your exposure to public wireless Internet environments and turning your wireless router off when not in use.

Body Products

What you put on your body is almost as important as what you put into your body. Allergens are caused by holding toxins in the body and your skin may be absorbing chemicals from a long list of products that are in common use but which could be the cause of issues for you. Do your own research on the following items and switch to natural or organic if you'd like to test the effects: sunscreen, make-up, body lotion, soap, shampoo, hair colorant, aftershave lotion, hair gels and sprays, perfumes, and deodorant all could contain potentially harmful chemicals to your body.

Household Products

The following items could also be a source for health issues: fabric softener sheets, air fresheners, stain guard sprays, deodorizer sprays, cleaners, and laundry soaps.

Building Materials

Construction materials and surfaces in your environment are also coming into the limelight as causing problems for some among us. If you have recently renovated or moved into a new home, the following items should not be overlooked. The most common problem sources are: paint, drywall, carpeting, floor finishes, pressure-treated wood, and insulation.

Water Quality

Something to check into? There is a scarcity of clean, fresh water sources on the planet today. Get your water checked for possible toxins, fertilizer, drug residue, bacteria, and unwanted minerals that are present or added.

Fitness and Exercise

Fresh air and exercise are important to good balanced health. How would you rate yourself in this department? Too much or not enough? Both are contributors to an unbalanced physical body.

Clothing

Your clothing can be a source for illness. Don't overlook the effects of modern fabrics that may stifle your energy or irritate your skin or even transfer an irritant into your body. My own personal experience is that I'm only comfortable in natural fabrics like silk, cotton, wool, hemp and leather. I feel like I'm "suffocating" in man-made fabrics.

Hidden Poisons

There are some harmful poisons in our lives, depending on one's degree of tolerance, that we don't seem to notice and some of these have the potential to cause havoc with our health. The chemicals used in nail care services and products are one such category that could be compromising your health. Another is vaccinations. For example, as Bonnie found, many immunizations contain preservatives such as mercury and formaldehyde and surprisingly today, autoimmune diseases are now being traced to vaccinations. Research has also indicated that encephalitis is an acknowledged medical reaction to many vaccinations.

Encephalitis is an acute inflammation of the brain and even a very mild form could lead to personality distortions and disorders. Other symptoms include headache, fever, confusion, drowsiness, and fatigue. More advanced and serious symptoms include seizures or convulsions, tremors, hallucinations, and memory problems.

A review of people surviving the encephalitis epidemics that swept America and Europe in the 1920's revealed that those who survived this condition would suffer from other various issues which were unheard of then but are recognized today as the following: ADD, ADHD, autism, Asperger's syndrome, anorexia, bulimia, impulsive violence, stuttering, mental retardation, dyslexia, sudden infant death syndrome, processing disorders, allergies, bed-wetting, Tourette's seizures, and sexual identity disorders.

Mercury, a Big Problem

Reflecting back on Bonnie's experience, we can see mercury is a particular concern. It has a very strong ability to mess up your entire system, which is part of the reason why mercury toxicity symptoms are so difficult to pin down. For example, some symptoms even relate to anxiety and depression. Mercury seems to have four main sources: dental amalgam fillings, vaccines, fish consumption and mercury pollution from coal-burning power plants. Ask yourself what your exposure is or has been to these four areas.

If you are experiencing any of the diseases or conditions mentioned above, you may wish to look into having a heavy metals test. If positive, check out the benefits of detoxification cleanses and chelation therapy. There are several methods that a doctor, naturopath or homeopath can assist with. There may also be lifestyle and dietary changes that can assist to reduce your exposure to harmful chemicals and metals to your body type.

Heavy Metal Toxicity: Common Symptoms

You may have heavy metal toxicity if you are experiencing any of these symptoms:

- Chronic pain throughout the muscles and tendons or any soft tissues of the body;
- Chronic malaise – general feeling of discomfort, fatigue, and illness;
- Brain fog – state of forgetfulness and confusion;
- Chronic infections such as Candida;
- Gastrointestinal complaints, such as diarrhea, constipation, bloating, gas, heartburn, and indigestion;
- Food allergies;
- Dizziness;
- Migraines and/or headaches;
- Visual disturbances;
- Mood swings, depression, and/or anxiety;

- Nervous system malfunctions – burning extremities, numbness, tingling, paralysis, and/or an electrifying feeling throughout the body.

Material World Check-list

The key to discovering causes of imbalance and irritation in your material world is to open up to all the possibilities, to audit every corner of your life for possible areas that may be causing or contributing to issues. Keep in mind that this journey is calling for change of some kind, not only in the physical environment, but in other areas of your life, to be explored in the coming chapters.

Exercise: Review Your Life

Review this list of items and rate yourself on how these could be affecting your health:

Exercise: Are you getting enough exercise to keep you healthy and to de-stress?

Water: Do you know what your water contains? Do you have a purification system?

Work: Exposure to obvious toxins and chemicals?

Air quality: Workplace location such as a sealed office tower.

Building materials: Carpeting, drywall, insulation, pressure-treated lumber and paints can be the source of issues.

Vehicle: Do you sit in traffic? Do you make long commutes?

Home: Have you inspected your residence recently?

Are there new building materials present?

Has there been any asbestos removed such as old floor tile?

How old is your furnace? Has it been checked for gas leaks?

Is your residence near or downwind from a busy road, farm, high tension wires, or factory (pollution, EMR)?

Soils: Some can contain lead and radium? This may be a problem source for gardeners and children.

EMR Electromagnetic radiation is causing issues among some people. How do you use your mobile device? Text or voice calling? Where do you carry your phone? Do you protect yourself from EMR while at your computer? Do you live or work near EMR sources like transformers, transmission wires, wireless devices and radio broadcast antennas?

Do you use cordless home phones?

Sun Tanning: Do you use a tanning salon? Is their equipment the latest technology?

Clothing: How do you feel in your present clothing choices? I suggest that you monitor this area as it is a subtle area that could be the source or contributor to a compound issue.

Body Products: Make a review of these.

Household Products and Cleaners: Review these as well.

Exposure to heavy metals such as mercury and lead.

My Life Environment Today
Here's a snapshot of my life at present.

Entertainment influences: Mostly comedy and how-to television with a little National Geographic thrown in. My reading material is spiritual, inspirational, economic and spy novels. The movies I see are usually comedy or light action adventure.

Spiritual practices: I have a daily half hour morning contemplation after breakfast to start my day, and an evening half hour contemplation with my wife after dinner. My reading material will often be a personal growth book on spiritual principles. On and off, I wear pharmaceutical gemstones to help me see areas in my life that need to change (see gemisphere.com) and to become aware of what areas of my life I need to purify in order to grow spiritually. The combination of contemplation, spiritual reading and being open to the nudges and inspiration of spirit is also key for me. Giving service to others is also vital to my spiritual growth.

Giving back: I love helping others understand key spiritual principles I have discovered through extensive volunteer work organizing and facilitating spiritual events in our community.

Exercise: I go to the gym two to three times a week, walk our dog daily and also play golf and ski about twice a week in season.

General lifestyle: I wear natural materials only. We cook with stainless steel, store left-over's in glass, and use the microwave only for heating up heating pads. In the summer, my wife preserves fresh picked fruits and vegetables which we enjoy all year.

Communications: I have shifted to using my cell phone only for emergencies, so it is off most of the time, and if on, never on or close to my body. I try to use a land line wherever possible while at home or working. I do not use cordless phones.

> *The doctor of the future will give no medicine but will interest his patients in the care of the human frame, in diet, and in the cause and prevention of disease.*
> Thomas Edison

Now let's take a look at what we are eating and how our health can be affected.

5
Our Passion for Harmful Foods

Today, more than 95% of all chronic disease is caused by food choice, toxic feed ingredients, nutritional deficiencies, and lack of physical exercise.

Mike Adams, The Health Ranger

Candice's Roller Coaster

Up until a couple of years ago Candice had been on what she called a sugar roller coaster ride for thirty-five years. She had been moving in and out of good health due to her addiction to sugar. She told me, "I had inflamed sinuses and yeast infections throughout my body. When I ate excessive amounts of sugar, I also had bad headaches and an overall feeling of lethargy combined with bouts of depression."

Candice explained, "Early on I had seen my medical doctor and she had first diagnosed my condition as low blood sugar and then later she confirmed that it was Candida Yeast. My doctor recommended I go off all foods with sugar including bread. Honey and fruit were okay in moderation. But I was addicted to sugar. I'd go off these harmful foods, then I'd start cheating and have just a little, and then the addiction for sugar would grow again.

"I lived like this for years. Then a couple of years ago I had an attack. I had eaten some chocolate bars and not soon after, my brain felt like it was on fire. It really scared me! It was the final straw after years of ups and downs on and off sugar and the terrible symptoms that would accompany my cheating. I realized I could do permanent damage – something really dangerous – so feeling my brain on fire was finally enough to get my attention to quit completely. I've now been sugar free for two years.

Another Issue to Deal With

"Recently I went in to see my Naturopathic Doctor to check my metal toxicity levels and the results were the best I've ever had. But then the doctor started asking me other questions. She inquired about a few things like, 'Do you eat out of a microwave?' My answers were negative but she revealed that my body was not absorbing vitamins and minerals and this would cause problems down the road. She told me that she suspected gluten intolerance and explained that the gluten could be causing an allergic reaction in my intestines. They would be inflamed as a result and then not be able to absorb the nutrients.

"I immediately accepted the gluten-free diet and I later found out even a crumb will weaken me, causing a severe reaction that would take several weeks to recover from; I discovered there was a bit of wheat in mixed nuts! Lately I've eliminated all processed foods and I'm eating a far healthier whole food diet. I even dine out less now and I feel great, happy, I have energy and I'm feeling like I'm loving life – not focussed on food.

A Larger Shift

"I had had many gentle nudges that I ignored, but when I was in the doctor's office, it all came into focus for me. This food shift has ushered in a new energy for me. I'm feeling much kinder and gentler these days and I've started reading a powerful series of books, The Ringing Cedars Series by Vladimir Megre, which talk about being more loving to Earth and promoting a whole new way of being. So this shift is on many levels and the departure from gluten has been a catalyst for a larger repositioning involving many changes. I've even decided to let go of my old first name which no longer fits me; I was called Candy and I've now softened it to Candice, my legal name.

"This whole change has also brought into focus for me how important every thought, feeling and action is and has moved me into a greater awareness of the present moment, and my impact on the world in every moment. It's shifted me toward being more loving and kind to everyone I meet and with whom I share my life.

"The healing process has made me realize how I need to purify myself on all levels, and to do this to be the most benefit to my planet, my world. I ask myself, 'How can I be better, more kind, more loving?'

"I'm looking for how I can open up a little more and impact life in a positive way."

∽

Life is a Moving Target

Like Candice, what you could eat in the past may be causing you issues today as you purify your being on all levels. Certain foods are known to cause problems in many people (e.g. gluten) and other foods may only affect a select few (peanuts). And then there are foods that have not been proven to cause any problems but may be a problem for you. (I have a problem with garlic.) Don't discount any possibilities. Life is a moving target! As you grow in vibration, many foods or food products may become incompatible in terms of resonance and therefore toxic in your body. This may start as a mild discomfort, progress to an irritation, and finally move to a very visible condition and outright pain. In other cases, there may be no direct signal at all, just a feeling of loss of energy, a malaise, or other subtle symptom that is not related to a particular action, product or food type. What I'm saying here is that you need to expect to make changes and that you may need to remove things from your sphere on a trial basis and monitor the effects. Let's start with a look at mass consumption foods.

Why Are We Such a Sick Society?

Despite the most advanced medical technology in the world, we are sicker than ever by nearly every measure. Two out of every three are overweight, cases of diabetes are exploding, especially in the younger population and about half are taking at least one prescription drug. Major medical operations have become routine, helping to drive health care costs to astronomical levels. Heart disease, Cancer and stroke are leading causes of death, even though billions are spent each year to "battle" these very conditions. Many others are dealing with a host of other degenerative diseases.

The China Study, a 20-year study that began in 1983 and was conducted jointly by the Chinese Academy of Preventive Medicine, Cornell University, and the University of Oxford examined mortality rates from 48 forms of Cancer and other chronic diseases. It concluded that counties in China with a high consumption of animal-based foods were more likely to have had higher death rates from "Western" diseases, while the opposite was true for counties that ate more plant foods. The study was conducted in those counties because they had genetically similar populations that tended, over generations, to live in the same way in the same place, and eat diets specific to those regions.

The conclusion: that most, if not all, of the degenerative diseases that afflict us can be controlled, or even reversed, by altering our present menu of animal-based and processed foods.

A Plant Strong Diet

Forks Over Knives is a recent video documentary that examined this thesis. Discoveries inspired by Doctors Campbell and Esselstyn, are examined and their years of groundbreaking studies presented. The documentary concluded that diseases like heart disease, type 2 diabetes, and even several forms of Cancer, can almost always be prevented—and in many cases reversed—by adopting a whole-foods, plant-based diet. These doctors recommend a plant-rich diet, scaling way back or eliminating altogether foods such as red meat, poultry, fish, and dairy products. Despite the profound implications of their findings, their work has remained relatively unknown to the public.

Results are reported as rapid and dramatic when a switch is made. Depending on your issues, you may wish to do your own three or four week test.

Heart Disease Findings

Dr. Dwight Lundell, a heart surgeon with 25 years experience, having performed over 5,000 open-heart surgeries, says inflammation is the primary cause of heart disease. He asks, "What are the biggest culprits of chronic inflammation? Quite simply, they are the overload of simple, highly processed carbohydrates (sugar, flour and all the products made from them) and the excess consumption of omega-6 vegetable oils like soybean, corn and sunflower that are found in many processed foods."

Maintaining Good Health

There are certain foods that could almost be called miracle foods, and they are all around us. What I find so tragic in our Western culture is that we have easy access to high-quality foods yet we are avoiding them in favour of convenience foods, processed foods and junk. Today's research is pointing out to us that just by adding some value-packed foods to our diet we can stay incredibly healthy well into our later years.

The excuse seems to be a shortage of time, yet these whole fresh foods I'm referring to can be made ready to eat in the same time as prepared and processed foods. I'm talking about steaming vegetables and making a simple salad for example. Or simply adding a miracle fruit like blueberries or a vitamin rich vegetable such as broccoli to your diet as part of a meal or as a snack. Again, I'm going to come back to the point that you are unique. You may not be able to tolerate in your diet what the masses can. You may need to augment your food choices with some highly nutritious foods if you are not already doing so. This is an easy place to make some critical changes!

What is Hidden Hunger?

The effects of hidden hunger can impair individuals, sapping their energy, productivity and mental ability. Hidden hunger is caused by a chronic lack of essential vitamins and minerals. People often don't realize they are suffering from hidden hunger and this can have potentially devastating effects. Hidden hunger can result from an overreliance on processed foods including fast foods and not eating fresh fruits and vegetables.

For example, a lack of Vitamin A can impair the immune system and make children more vulnerable to diseases such as measles, diarrhea, and malaria. A fetus or infant that suffers from iodine deficiency may become mentally impaired. A lack of iron can cause anaemia in women and children and mental impairment in growing children. Women who do not have enough folic acid are more likely to become anaemic and to have children with neural tube birth defects.

Micronutrients

Micronutrients are now becoming better known as essential to good health. These nutrients are required by humans and other living things in small quantities throughout life to orchestrate a whole range of physiological functions, but which the organism itself cannot produce.

Micronutrients are needed only in minuscule amounts, yet can be considered miracle elements that enable the body to produce enzymes, hormones and other substances essential for proper growth and development. As tiny as the amounts are, however, the consequences of their absence are severe. Iodine, Vitamin A and iron are most important in terms of our health. Other micronutrients include chromium, copper, manganese, selenium, zinc and molybdenum.

Dr. Joel Fuhrman is a big proponent of micronutrients and recommends the following six "super foods" to be included in a healthy diet: salad greens, onions, mushrooms, beans, berries, and seeds. Others say these foods are also Cancer inhibiting foods. Dr. Fuhrman's suggestion is to eat a salad every day with these ingredients for optimum health. What could be simpler!

Vitamin E

Vitamin E is another essential for good health. Processed foods, alcohol, tobacco, and smog increase your need for Vitamin E. Fatigue, stress and pollution can deplete it. Heat, oxygen, freezing and chlorine destroys Vitamin E.

Foods that are rich in Vitamin E include seeds, nuts, soy beans, brown rice, oats, fresh wheat germ and free range eggs. Also beneficial are dark green leafy vegetables, Brussels sprouts and broccoli.

Antioxidants

Antioxidants (anti-oxygen) are your first line of defence against free radicals. Free radicals are a normal part of metabolism and play a vital role in many biochemical processes, but they must be kept under control. To counteract these radical oxidants, the brain needs an ample supply of antioxidants. Basically, antioxidants are molecules that free radicals find more attractive than our body's cellular components.

Antioxidants can be found in micronutrients obtained from food. There are many different kinds of micronutrients that function as antioxidants to neutralize, or quench, free radicals. Each works in a unique manner and has a particular area of focus, but they also complement each other in an extraordinary synergy that effectively controls free radicals.

United States Department of Agriculture (USDA) nutritionists examined more than 100 different kinds of fruits, vegetables, nuts, spices, cereals and other foods for their antioxidant content. The results weren't altogether surprising: fruits, vegetables and beans claimed all the spots.

Here are the USDA top 20 antioxidant foods:

1. Small red bean (dried),
2. Wild blueberry,
3. Red kidney bean (dried)
4. Pinto bean,
5. Blueberry (cultivated),
6. Cranberry,
7. Artichoke (cooked hearts),
8. Blackberry,
9. Prune,
10. Raspberry,
11. Strawberry,
12. Red delicious apple,
13. Granny Smith apple,
14. Pecan,
15. Sweet cherry,
16. Black plum,
17. Russet potato,
18. Black bean (dried),
19. Plum,
20. Gala apple.

The number one antioxidant-rich food, small red beans (dried), at the top of the list are sometimes called a Mexican red bean, but they are actually only grown in Washington, Idaho, and Alberta, Canada.

A Source of Potential Health Problems

In today's world of chemical agriculture, too many fertilizers herbicides and insecticides can play mayhem with our bodies allowing free radicals to attack us.

Today's large-scale farming methods and many genetically modified foods necessitate farmers use fertilizers, insecticides and herbicides to produce crop yields at competitive prices. It's a highly competitive business. Unfortunately, these chemicals end up in our food. Of course "everyone" is eating these foods but as previously discussed, your personal tolerance to these unwanted chemical residues may be lower than the average person's ability to resist their effects.

Here are some foods to monitor for your own ability to assimilate and remain in good health, or to buy organic: apples, celery, strawberries, peaches, spinach, nectarines (imported), grapes (imported), sweet bell peppers, potatoes, blueberries, lettuce, kale, collard greens, apricots, green beans and cherries.

Soy Products – Are They a Problem for You?

Numerous studies have found that food products containing soy can affect the health of some people. In North America soybeans are typically grown with pesticides and herbicides as most crops are genetically modified. If you are having health issues such as a thyroid disorder, kidney stones, and food allergies, as in all issues you are dealing with, I encourage you to do your own research on the Internet etc.

Obesogens, Hidden Causes of Weight Gain

"Obesogen" is a relatively new term that has emerged to describe a substance or food that contributes in some way to increased weight gain or obesity. An obesogen is a natural or synthetic chemical that is an endocrine-disruptor. Simply put, these chemicals disrupt the function of hormonal systems and metabolism, leading to weight gain. Obesogens enter our bodies different ways:

• Hormones given to animals;
• Plastics in food and drink packaging;
• Ingredients added to processed food; and
• Pesticides sprayed on produce.

Obesogens can cause damage because they mimic human hormones such as estrogen, they miss-program stem cells to be fat cells and they can possibly alter gene functions.

The Top Six Obesogens

High Fructose Corn Syrup is an ingredient in many packaged and processed foods. The main problem is that because it is so abundant and so cheap, it has found its way even into foods like pretzels and hamburger buns.

Animal and Fish Protein. In many animals, obesogens are stored in their fat. Be aware of some Atlantic and Farm-Raised fish which can have more pesticides in them and be artificially colored to look like wild salmon.

Tap Water. Because of the pesticides used in farming, those pesticides seep into the soil and the water table below. The best way to prevent these obesogens getting into your drinking water is to use a granular activated carbon (GAC) filter for your water purification. Also check your municipal water supplier for their water quality report to see what's in your water.

Things around your house that contain obesogens. First is Bisphenol A or BPA a synthetic estrogen found in many plastics. This has been banned from baby bottles for years, but canned baby formula is lined inside the can with BPA. Also fatty and acidic foods that come in cans are lined with BPA, like tomato products and tuna. Experts recommend purchasing tuna in pouches that do not contain BPA and limiting the tomato products to those in jars or to do your own canning of tomato products. The other things to be conscious of are hard plastic water bottles with #7 in the triangle stamped on the bottom. Never microwave in containers made of plastic. BPA-free plastics contain triangles on the bottom with numbers 1, 2, 4, 5 and 6. Plastics with numbers 3 or 7 have no guarantee that they do not contain BPA.

Perfluorooctanoic acid or PFOA is another concern found in the home. It is a substance that makes things non-stick on pots, pans and cooking utensils. PFOA can impact your thyroid gland. One suggestion is to use wooden utensils for cooking because metal can scrape the coating which can end up in your food. PFOA is also found in microwave popcorn and pizza delivery boxes.

Also, be aware of **polyvinyl chloride or PVC** which release phthalates which lower testosterone and lowers metabolism so fat cannot be burned efficiently. These are found on vinyl shower curtains, especially liners. When taking a shower, combined with hot water, you are in a phthalate bath and inhaling this substance. Meat from the supermarket wrapped in see-through plastic wrap is loaded with PVC in the industrial/commercial strength, but home use wrap is not. I suggest going to a butcher who will wrap your meat in brown paper instead.

North American wheat is now coming under examination. According to Cardiac Specialist Doctor William Davis, author of *Wheat Belly*, it can now be a major contributor to weight gain and a large belly.

When I stopped eating wheat I dropped ten pounds and lost my belly. I substituted coconut flour bread, one hundred percent rye bread, and rice pasta and more recently I have been baking my own eight grain bread. While travelling in Asia, South America and Europe, I have found that these local wheat food products do agree with my system.

Other areas to research that could be hidden contributors to weight gain are alcohol, hydrogenated oils (coconut oil and olive oils are good alternatives), food additives and fast foods. So be aware of the things that can hinder your metabolism and hurt you and your family.

Food Additives, Another Area of Concern

Used primarily to preserve shelf life and boost flavour, as well as to maintain colour, many synthetic additives have undergone inadequate, conflicting or inconclusive testing. While none of them has been definitively proven to be harmful, they haven't been proven to be safe, either; so being the unique being that you are, some additives may not be contributing to your good health.

A good website for doing your own research is *Center for Science in the Public Interest*. For the Center's complete list of additives and their accompanying safety rating visit the food safety section of its website.

The real message is that if you are having health challenges, try to eliminate foods with additives from your diet, even if for a test period and eat only fresh fruits, vegetables and meats. Monitor the results for a month of two, keeping a record of how you feel in your journal each day.

Gluten, a Hidden Cause of Health Issues

Many people today are suffering from issues that their doctors are unable to diagnose. These include migraine or headaches, joint pains or aches, brain fog, frequent bloating or gas, IBS, acid reflux, diarrhea or chronic constipation, depression or anxiety, ongoing fatigue and chronic eczema or acne. Dr. Oz (at doctoroz.com) says four or more symptoms indicate that gluten may be impacting your health. But even one symptom, if severe and chronic, like Candice experienced, can be a sign of gluten sensitivity. You may want to consult your doctor or easier yet, try going gluten-free for 2-4 weeks. Gluten free means eliminating wheat, rye and barley from your diet. Good substitutes include rice pasta and rice flour or coconut flour bread as I have mentioned and added to my diet.

Your pH Balance

What you are eating could also be throwing off your body's pH balance into the acidic range. It is not healthy to be too acidic (nor too alkaline for that matter). pH represents the balance of positively charged (acid-forming) ions to negatively charged (alkaline forming) ions in your body. A low pH means you are too acidic. For optimum health your body should be slightly alkaline, however most North Americans are too acidic due to emotional and physical stress and the foods being consumed. This can cause toxic build-up, lack of absorption of important minerals and vitamins and free radical oxidation resulting in frequent colds and flu, weight gain, poor hair and skin and low bone density. More seriously, doctors have linked acidity with the proliferation of cancer cells. An alkaline pH discourages cancer development.

Key things to be aware of that cause acidity in the body include a strong reliance on processed foods, alcoholic beverages, sugars, hard and processed cheese, artificial sweeteners and red meat. Your local health food store can provide you with lots of suggestions for testing and balancing your pH levels.

Making Changes

You might be saying, what's next? How can I start making changes? There are a few simple things you can commit to, that require little will-power or sacrifice. Implement the common sense actions below recommended by a host of experts, and you are bound to improve your health and maintain it.

1. Keep fruits like apples and bananas out on your counter. You'll be more likely to eat them if you have to look at them every day!

2. Eat a salad every day for lunch or with every meal. Make it a rule. It doesn't matter what you are eating, just get a side salad. Skip the dressing if you can and just squeeze a little lemon juice and salt/pepper on top or balsamic vinegar and oil.

3. Focus on adding nutrient dense foods, instead of subtracting unhealthy food from your diet. It is easier to add than subtract. Over time, you will get used to eating the leafy greens, and find it easier to cut back on your serving of processed foods.

4. Avoid refined sugars.

5. Drink lots of water.

> *It's bizarre that the produce manager is more important to my children's health than the pediatrician.*
>
> Meryl Streep, Actor and Singer

Exercise: Making Beneficial *Changes*

What food can you give up that is potentially harmful to you now or in the future?

Write down one thing that you can let go of that is no longer serving your best health interests - e.g. refined sugars, a food additive, hydrogenated oils, chemical sugar substitutes, wheat.

Letting Go of Certain Foods

My own personal journey has been one of letting go of certain foods for the last thirty years as I discovered one-by-one they made me feel ill or negatively affected me in some way. In my teens, I let go of chocolate. In my twenties I terminated refined sugars and all the confectionary foods and drinks I consumed. In my thirties, I had to drop coffee and alcohol and became vegetarian. A few years later, I added back into my diet fish and poultry. In my forties I added back in red meat after being diagnosed as borderline anaemic, revealed in a live blood cell analysis. I also let go of juices and started to only drink water. In my fifties, I had to let go of wheat due to bloating in my belly. I also discovered that I had a genuine sensitivity to MSG. I started to get a red flare above my lip if I ingested just a small amount of this substance. In recent years I've had to let go of eggs, snack foods with hydrogenated oil and garlic, and I can only tolerate milk if it is organic.

As I'm writing this book, my wife and I are now cutting back our meat consumption and emphasizing fresh organic vegetables and fruits in our diets. We have also purchased a new gravity-fed water filter system that produces natural alkaline water.

Foods have been a moving target for me and as indicated above, I have had to reverse myself in the meat department. With all of the changes that I've made I'm still grateful for the many foods I can still enjoy, but I'm careful not overindulge in any one particular food which could create an imbalance. The key for me is being open to what my body is telling me and making the changes, often with experimentation to be sure I was doing the right thing. These changes are the price of good health and spiritual growth.

Exercise: Review Your Diet

Review the following and rate yourself on how these could be affecting your health:

Substances: Wine, beer, alcohol, drinks containing caffeine and recreational substances will affect your journey at some point. Be prepared to make changes here!

Drinks: Soda pop, coffee, tea, fruit juices, milk – many of these are exposed to pesticides and possibly herbicides and many carry levels of sugar which could be causing you problems.

Foods: Do you buy processed foods?

What ingredients/additives do these contain?

Foods around the store perimeter like meats, vegetables, fruit, and dairy tend to be better for us than processed foods but you may need to determine what exposure they have had to chemicals at source or in processing.

Processed meat products are loaded with ingredients that could be harmful to your unique constitution.

Don't overlook gluten and the obesogens previously mentioned.

Microwave: Do you microwave your food or beverages? There is controversy about what microwaving does to food and water. As the unique being that you are, this could be a source of problems for you.

My Diet at Present

Here is a snapshot of my food and beverages at present:

Key dietary influences: I only drink filtered tap water. I use almond beverage on my cereal, a home-made granola that I eat with previously frozen berries each morning preceded by a grapefruit. I have a mid-morning piece of toast, home-made from eight grain cereal and coconut flour that is wheat free. I've had to drop North American wheat from my diet and substitute rice, rye or other grains. I eat lots of salads mostly at lunchtime and I eat red meat, chicken and fish but the portions are small. My wife and I are trending toward eating organic, particularly the high risk fruits and vegetables.

My favorite snacks: mixed nuts and home-made spelt flour crackers.

Foods I have left behind: garlic, eggs, wheat (North American), sugar, tea and coffee, most foods containing additives, preservatives and hydrogenated oils.

Most noticeable beneficial addition: coconut oil – I use it on my skin as an aftershave and sun screen, on my morning toast and as a cooking oil.

My goal in writing this chapter has been to highlight several foods, food groups and additives that could be causing problems for you and give you some ideas where you can begin to easily make changes, taking charge of your health. As said before, you are unique and your sensitivities are as well. What others are able to eat can be causing you issues, so feel free to experiment and selectively add or subtract foods from your diet and monitor the way you feel a few weeks at a time. And remember, from a spiritual view-point, life is a purification process.

Life expectancy would grow by leaps and bounds if green vegetables smelled as good as bacon.

Doug Larson, Newspaper Columnist

Now let's take a look at accidents from the perspective of what they can teach us and the spiritual healings (purification) they can usher in.

6

The Spiritual Gifts of Accidents

On the occasion of every accident that befalls you, remember to turn to yourself and inquire what power you have for turning it to use.

Epictetus, Greek Philosopher

Jill's Crash Course in Self-discovery

Jill's awakening began the moment she regained consciousness in the crumpled body of a small commercial aircraft embedded in the side of a mountain. I'll let her tell her story in her own words. (I've taken the liberty to insert some quotes from Jill's book, *My 'Plane' Truth*, as headlines in her short overview.)

...On January 21, 2006, my husband and I were enjoying a couple's massage during a romantic getaway and five hours later we were experiencing fifteen terrifying minutes of uncertainty as to whether we would live or die. The single engine plane suddenly lost all its power and the fate and destiny of all eight passengers on board was about to change forever. Flashing before me was my life... what had I done? What and who would I miss? More importantly, what was the meaning of those unfamiliar blue eyes that superimposed themselves over my husband's eyes minutes before we crashed? I somehow had a knowingness that I would survive and yet a feeling that Terry, my husband wouldn't.

**I knew the moment we crashed there must be a
much bigger reason for my surviving.**

This true story appears to be about the miraculous rescue, my survival, and of the trauma of losing Terry and my 'princess' life as I knew it. Buried deep beneath the many layers of truth, the real 'soul' story emerges... which is of my spiritual transformation towards a life that I had thought was possible but had no idea how to get there. All of which had nothing to do with my material world that I had aspired to for most of my life. The spiritual path that I had been catapulted onto was certainly uplifting, unfamiliar and yet fascinating to me. I was 47, widowed and had a clean slate to begin my life over again. Undaunted by the magnitude of this tragedy, I took the road of uncertainty over despair. My long journey from recovery first began with the eleven operations required to put humpty dumpty back together again. In fact, however, it was the emotional body that needed the most healing and where the reason for this accident began to unfold very clearly for me.

Meditation became a very effective tool for me: simply being quiet and listening to the universe and to myself enabled me to observe what wave I was riding on at the moment.

My journey inward in search of answers began by learning to meditate. Only because of the lengthy recovery time required was I able to see how perfect everything was - divinely inspired if you will. I needed that time to listen to what my soul had been trying all my life to get me to hear and see. My busy mind and Type A personality was not accustomed to slowing down, nor was I open to listening with my heart instead of my head. However, I soon learned that in the quiet state of mind... was where soul really spoke to me. During at least eighteen months of the total four years it took for my physical healing time, I was in this altered state of consciousness in which everything around me was coming from a state of LOVE. This state was so unusual and unfamiliar to me, particularity given the nature of this tragedy, that this time I knew I had to listen.

My fears had nothing to do with crashing in an airplane, but rather a much bigger picture that involved a lot of my own limiting beliefs about everything: men, position, trust, and of course my own self-worth.

As I peeled away the layers of some very deep-seated emotions like anger, resentment, and disappointment, I discovered that many of my beliefs that were valid and true for me before the accident were now on the table for questioning. I very much felt the 'disconnect' between my old thoughts and my new feelings.

I could see that some of these old behaviours, resulting from my subconscious limiting beliefs did not serve me anymore. The accident acted as a catalyst to allow me to see my truth and to take responsibility for my life. And when I changed how I perceived things, the things I perceived changed. For example, my body would heal and function optimally if I let go of the points of view that caused all my discomfort in the first place. When my anger and frustration diminished, my bowel irritability improved. And once I let go of carrying the weight of the world on my shoulders, my neck, back and shoulders stopped aching. Only when I perceived the accident as a gift did my body start to function with more ease.

Because of this heightened awareness, I also became aware of my dreams that were also leading me to my truth. Coincidentally and synchronystically, all the right people, places and things were simply lining up for me, to not only heal but more importantly to help me realize that I was meant to survive this accident, despite great odds, because there was something 'more' and 'bigger' for me to still do and or be.

My near death experience in the plane was when my soul was contemplating whether I should/could transition now OR, did I still have some unfinished business with regards to the contract that I had written before I even incarnated into this body. Having found the owner of "those eyes" in a new relationship, God had shown me how to gently open my heart again to love. My dreams gently suggested I start to look at all the events in my life, from childhood on, that led up to the accident. There are no accidents and there are no exceptions. So, given that Universal truth, I had to find a way to make sense of it all. After all, bad things don't happen to good people!

Before the crash I led with my brain, but this accident was helping me realize, in order to be happy and find true peace and harmony I needed to lead with my heart.

All my life, God has been whispering and nudging me along towards my true purpose... only I never listened. My lengthy recovery allowed me time to connect all the dots, as I examined every inch of my life. In doing so, I discovered many limiting beliefs about myself that were not going to serve me any longer in my expanded awareness of who I really was. I also discovered my 'shadow' self, the parts of my personality that I hadn't wanted to admit to, but in fact were true. When I faced my controlled and bullied childhood I learned to forgive my transgressors, for whom I had held so much silent anger inside of me, and to forgive them for all they had done to me. In fact, I also learned to forgive myself for allowing it to fester in my later years. Up until the accident, I had suffered in angry silence. I never spoke up and I didn't think I had anything important to say.

I also made the connections between the parts of my body that were injured and the parts afterwards that continued to not be in balance as to what I was still holding onto. My emotional body was speaking the loudest. When I didn't let go of my anger, I had trouble digesting my food and was constipated a lot, despite my now more active schedule and healthy eating. I felt out of balance in my lower chakras (energy centers) which I was now able to see when I meditated. Once I could make those connections, I worked on that particular issue that related to that chakra.

Our reactions to life-altering events are what make us either victims or victors in life. There are no accidents and there are no exceptions.

Through the excavation of all my stuff, I discovered that addictions and limiting beliefs are carried in the cellular memory in our DNA. This is why on a subconscious level we continue to attract the same types of people and situations into our lives – unless we are willing to look at these limiting beliefs about ourselves and take the necessary steps to change those beliefs. Until I was willing to look inside and change my limiting and negative beliefs, I would stay stuck in circumstances that would play out not only in this lifetime, but possibly every lifetime still to come.

Having the courage to change our perspectives and our limiting beliefs is not easy, but is each soul's journey – and it is worth it. It is a process and a journey all at the same time.

Each step of the way of recovery beautifully laid out for me some karmic lessons I needed to learn and address in this lifetime.

Challenging everything I once knew and believed, faith... a now knowingness of not only who I am as personality, but that we are simply souls having a human experience on Earth, and not a human having the occasional soulful experience. The other side is simply filled with unconditional love, acceptance, joy, peace, happiness and creativity. My new found faith allowed me to take the unfamiliar steps towards my authentic self and thus allowing me peace and freedom from this tragedy and more. I mostly heard... love more and simplify my life. Love and forgive myself and others for exactly who they are. It took a life threatening event and near death experience to see this truth... I call my "plane" truth.

Jill Douglas has documented her healing journey in her book, My "Plane" Truth.

∼

Accidents Lead Us Through Change

Accidents and resulting injury are another way we are led through change in this physical world and in Jill's case into a whole new way of being. Jill shows us how accidents serve a purpose in moving us forward spiritually, teaching us something we didn't know about ourselves, otherwise we would not need the message(s) and lesson(s) contained in the experience.

Accidents can range from minor cuts and bruises, to a bump on the head, to a major "train wreck." These incidents are spiritual wake-up calls and can be seen as spiritual gifts – a call of Soul to make changes in our perceptions, how we view life. Know that everything that is happening is a result of choices we've made in the past - karma. Perhaps you have left the tracks in thought, word and deed and are now off course from your destiny. You may have, at the point of the accident, reversed your path, ignored previous "messages" and therefore need a reminder or even a time-out to help get back on to your true agenda as Soul.

Like illness and disease, accidents are an opportunity to discover something new about yourself. My story is a prime example of Soul wanting to bring something to the surface. In my case, the message needed to be repeated for it to sink in.

A Spiritual Wake-up Call

Several years ago I was playing racquetball and crashed to the floor with a loud cracking sound. I thought at first that the floor was cracked and I was actually crawling around on the floor looking for the broken board. When I stood up my leg was not right. I couldn't finish the game as I was not able to walk properly. Later that day I still hadn't recovered full use of my leg so I checked into the hospital. Diagnosis: ruptured Achilles tendon. I was placed in a cast for ten weeks while the tendon knitted itself back together.

This was a major event as it affected my mobility at a time when my business consultancy was having challenges: I hadn't signed a new client project for months, I was borrowing money just to survive, and my wife and company operating partner was showing up in our home office later and later each day, over-exercising, and losing too much weight in the process. Our relationship was strained and overall my life was the pits!

There Was More to Come

Ten weeks later in the dead of winter, I was cut out of the cast and began walking carefully. The following day, I ended up in hospital - again: I had re-ruptured my tendon. I faced another cast and eight weeks of limited mobility. When I got home, despondent, my wife said, "I guess there is never a good time for anything, but I'm leaving." Suddenly a bad day turned into the worst day of my life! I didn't see it coming – yet all the signs were there.

It took me another year to see how perfectly arranged this ordeal was laid out. I needed to move on (legs move us forward) and so did she. I needed to see that we had learned all that we could in this lifetime together in the relationship, and it was time for changes.

Resolving Past-life Karma

There was a strong karmic pattern that needed to be resolved in this life. I was shown in contemplation several months later, a past life where the seeds of this long drawn-out experience took place. In that moment of heightened awareness, I was shown a vision of a life in which I was an Indian brave with a wife and young child. In that setting I had a very strong urge to go off on a vision quest in spite of the fears and objections of my wife. I never returned and she was left with the young child and a life of hardship. In this life, I cared for our young child for a time until she found a new direction, re-balancing the scales of karmic justice.

Slowing down, spending eighteen weeks in leg casts allowed me to see and accept the changes that entered all parts of my life in the months that followed.

Accident Messages

Accidents, these unexpected gifts of guidance, can drop in out-of-the-blue to alter the course of our life in small or dramatic ways. A couple I know literally met by accident when his car hit hers on a highway. They've been married now for over thirty years.

What I've come to know is that one needs to pay special attention to any event that happens more than once. Also, look for patterns and themes found inside events. Like dreams, quite often the "accident" messages we receive are symbolic and need to be interpreted in light of what is going on in our life. If you meet resistance in what you are doing, this is your opportunity to re-think choices you have made or a direction you have taken.

Exercise: Learning from Accidents

Every near mishap and calamity is an opportunity – to see it as guidance in your life. Even the smallest cut or bruise can help you fine-tune your life, so if you experience a setback or accident, ask yourself:

What could this mean?

What is going on in my life this could be related to?

What was I thinking about or doing at the time of the accident that could be telling me something I need to know or change?

Has this occurred before (like a bump, cut, a near fall or even car accident)?

Now let's take a look at our spiritual make-up in more detail to see where the other areas of healing can be found.

Part III

Cleaning Out Disharmonies in Our Spiritual Bodies

Disharmonies occur in our bodies, setting us on a path of purification from outmoded physical, emotional and mental habits and also patterns from our past.

7

Roadmap to Your Spiritual Bodies

All changes, even the most longed for, have their melancholy; for what we leave behind us is a part of ourselves; we must die to one life before we can enter another.

Anatole France, Nobel Prize winner for literature

Dustin's Awakening

Eighteen months prior to our meeting, Dustin had landed in Children's Hospital fighting for his life with third degree burns to his face, neck, shoulders, hands and arms. The day started out as one filled with adventure with his buddies, on a hike to a canyon with an amazing waterfall. They had hiked up to the canyon and then used a rope to ascend a two-hundred-and-fifty foot drop to the canyon floor, quite an adventure for fourteen-year-olds.

Dustin described himself and his friends as "a bunch of pyromaniacs." They built a small fire at the bottom to celebrate. They had the fire lit, barely, and they wanted to juice up the flames. As Dustin held a dimly lit torch, his friend held a water bottle full of gasoline. Dustin asked his friend to spray some gas on the torch. Their adventure suddenly turned to horror!

Dustin was engulfed in a whoosh of gas-fired flames and the brush behind him even caught fire. "I took off running and for twenty seconds I was trying to pat out the flames and get them off my face, neck and chest," he told me. "Running only accelerated the flames. My friend told me to get in the river, but I hesitated because I knew it was glacial. However, I was in so much severe pain, I jumped in. The frigid water cooled the flames out. When I came back to my friends they saw half my face was missing! My face, hands and neck were severely burned – it looked like my body was skinned. My lungs and throat were also singed. With so much adrenalin going, I wrapped my hands in cloth and, using the rope, scaled up the two-hundred-fifty-foot canyon wall to the top. My friend called his sister who came and drove us to the hospital."

In the hospital Dustin's singed throat began to swell shut and he entered into critical condition. He was stabilized and air ambulanced to a major Children's Hospital. During the next three days, Dustin faced life and death issues including low blood pressure and then a bad lung infection. At this point, he began to lose his fight to live. "I felt tired, defeated and was living with mild sedation and a breathing tube stuck down my neck, he recounted. My situation was weighing on me."

Awakening to a Higher Consciousness of Being

"A few days later when the tube came out I had a profound experience – an awakening of gratitude. Even though my face looked like a pig's ear dog treat, I reached an acceptance of my condition and that I was not going to die. I felt an amazing appreciation for listening to music, drinking water again, having a chocolate shake – everything became so peaceful for me. It was awesome to breathe without that tube. I felt deep gratitude for all the little things and for being alive – I was excited to be alive versus just being in a body!"

Now it was time for Dustin to heal. Dustin spent six days in the hospital and then was sent home to live in a sterile environment. He had weekly journeys back to the hospital for the next four weeks. Dustin was told he would need skin grafts to repair the severe damage, yet as I sat opposite Dustin eighteen months later during our chat, he had no visible signs of the burns!

Creative Visualization and a Positive Attitude

Dustin explained, "I never let the idea of getting an infection or having any other issues even enter my mind. I deeply believed this could not happen and that I would heal normally. I held a very positive outlook. I had a saying, 'I'm going to have such a healing day. These scars are going to just fade away.' I didn't see myself as being too physically changed. I thought myself well. In spite of what I was told, I never bought into how bad it could be. I would put on music and meditate/contemplate and see myself well. I would intend – watching my skin repair – kinda like mindfulness. I maintained this level of inspiration and hope."

It was during the healing months that Dustin was introduced to a spiritual woman by a family friend. He told me, "I just knew we had met in a past life. When I went into her shop, I was so drawn to her. She looked at me and told me I have a healing vibe. We became friends very quickly and I trusted her. Since our meeting, all of my wisdom has come from her – she answers a lot of my questions. She's been a catalyst for my spiritual evolution and I speak to her every few days. She's like a mentor.

A New Passion for Serving Others

"Shortly after meeting her, I was attracted to Reiki (a form of therapy where the practitioner channels energy into a patient to encourage healing) after being introduced to it by a buddy. Reiki felt like meeting an old friend. It has come naturally and I felt like I had done this a lot in past lives."

Dustin told me, "We exist physically and Reiki is like energetic water – it works on all four levels: physically, emotionally, mentally and spiritually. Reiki is humble. It is not associated with any religion. Whenever I have a 'dis-ease' on any of the four levels, I'll give myself a session. So my healing process from the burns has led me to Reiki and my understanding of reality now – the nature of reality. I connect with this. I'm even building a Reiki room in our house.

"I'm on a journey of uncovering. I now see the light and love in everyone. I see things as they are, and people as they are. I'm no better than anyone else."

Dustin's awakening has affected his whole family who have now discovered contemplation/meditation and are supporting Dustin with his spiritual choices and explorations.

Dustin says his daily meditations/contemplations have helped him immensely. "When I contemplate, I have this knowingness. I just feel it to validate it. I'm trying to go with the experiential aspect to get at truth. I like a lot of the words Buddha spoke about experiencing it for yourself as opposed to religious propaganda. I do a lot of visualization and with healing on the four levels, I use it experientially. We have this persona, but I release this and just experience a true nature of reality."

When I asked Dustin if he had received guidance, intuition, insights or a feeling of love or protection, he replied: "Yes. My way of asking for help is I contact my higher self, as long as I'm not resisting the natural way of being. I don't limit my love to anybody or anything. I see their light." Dustin went on to say, "I'm at level three Reiki now – incorporating it into daily life. I don't care about the opinions of others. I don't have any say in their beliefs. Where they're at on their journey is their business. I respect all religions. For example, I'll use any religious symbol people are comfortable with in Reiki treatments. Everybody is One in the field of Love. I like the saying, 'Everybody smiles in the same language.'"

New Realizations

Exploring his spiritual experiences, we talked about some of his new realizations. "What I think is we have a contract. The fire and burns have taken me to a happy place where I'm meant to be. There is no limit on age regarding spiritual growth. (Dustin is sixteen today.) The element of fire is related to spirit and now I feel I'm going down a spiritual path. Awakening comes in all forms and in many ways. I believe we incarnate to learn lessons we couldn't learn in spirit form. Not being resistant to anything is key. Ignorance is the deepest poison – it is the main resistance. I'll help anybody who needs it, when they are ready for it."

As you can see, Dustin has undergone a spiritual transformation since the fire, but is also a work in progress. Dustin added, "I always know what's best for me, and if not, I go inside, inquiring within a contemplation/meditation. With any 'dis-ease' I'll use Reiki."

When it comes to the emotional level, Dustin says, "I've come to see it for what it is. I'm not bound by this physical body. These negative emotions are not relevant. Mind is always searching for physical items to fill it – old beliefs and thought patterns. The ego mind is resistance to flow. But the ego is something we are always going to be working on – to be forgiving and accepting of other people. There will always be unnecessary emotions. Kindness settled in for me when I realized we are all One. I'll speak up if I see an unkindness."

I asked Dustin what he feels he has learned since his encounter with fire. First, he offered, "My injury was an awakening for me. I see a lot of changes in myself. I'm emotionally a lot more stable today. Spiritually, I'm not going to say anything... it would be limited by words. I'll help anyone with a spiritual issue or a question. My favourite expression these days is: 'It's not as hard as you think.' This is what I tell people. Friends come to me and I give good advice by stepping out of the mud of the situation and seeing the bigger picture. If people make fun of me, I see it for what it is. I've moved from material values to spiritual values now and this has brought a big shift in perceptions and awareness."

Three Inspiring Messages

The biggest realizations for Dustin have come at an incredibly young age for him. He told me his most recent discovery is, "We are all One. I was told this, but I now know this to be true. It was mental before, but through experiences, I know. Everything is life-force energy – it is Love. Source energy, the Divine, that's what we are. Whatever sport you are playing, we are all on the same field."

Dustin's second realization is: "Everything is perfect as it is."

His third awakening is: "Everything is changing. Resistance to change is disharmonious, and this translates itself into disease." Dustin talked again about his love for Reiki: "I love working with Reiki. It works on all four levels of existence. The patient does the healing; Reiki supplies the patient with what's in their highest and best interest."

I asked Dustin what he would say to readers of this book - if he could offer any words of advice. "Love," he said. "I was so damaged and yet I met my highest excitement and love when that tube came out of my throat. There was no limit to the feeling of this love flowing through me. The Source is Love, Peace, and cycling it through. With the experiences I've had, I can hardly define it in words – it's so intimate and natural. I like the statement, 'Silence is the language of the Gods and everything else is just a bad translation.'"

Your Personal Journey

Our lesson plan is unique to each of us and therefore our journey is also personal to us. We come into this life with our particular characteristics, qualities, genetic make-up and conditions which form the basis of our lifetime adventure. This is called karma, a lifetime package of the seeds of our lessons. Whether we consciously realize it or not, our journey is one of growing and purification and our mission is to eventually become a co-worker with the Creator or God, serving life.

This journey of life is a path of purification, to release more and more of that which no longer serves our wellbeing, to become better and better. This "better" can be described as the manifestation of

God-like qualities - to become more compassionate, kinder, respectful, forgiving, patient, and of course, loving in a spiritual way. To love all life, all of God's creatures and to treat all life as God treats Its dominions is our eventual goal. And so our lesson plan, our challenges are before us to move us along our personal path to purification.

Discovering the Underlying Threads of Imbalance

We humans seem to learn the best when times are the toughest, when our backs are to the wall so to speak. Illness, injury and other challenges can certainly put us there. Pain, whether it is physical, emotional or mental is said to be a great teacher. But we can move through these conditions and back into harmony and balance by healing ourselves in a spiritual way. By this I mean, to take exploratory measures to discover the root cause or causes of our lack of purity that has come to the fore. We need to find the source of the problem, the disharmony that we have created or found ourselves in, to determine our way back to balance. The problem is that these causes are often a part of our very nature and need to be uncovered. After all, we have lived with ourselves for a long time and are quite used to our make-up. But to be in dis-ease or ill-at-ease there is something we need to change. This is the key. Our disease or accident is telling us there is a need for change.

The process is about taking responsibility for our current condition, and taking action to discover the underlying threads of imbalance. Of course one can say I caught a cold, or a bug, or this or that condition just happened out of the blue. Or I was brought up in a dysfunctional family or in a bad community. But once you decide that you want to take charge of your life, these thought patterns give way to ones that say: What can I do about this? What can I learn about this? What is this teaching me? Of course a bug or genetics or other "medically" defined cause is present, however when you are open to examining the spiritual dimension, you can uncover what caused the imbalance that allowed the condition to manifest. After all, our bodies are filled with bugs, bacteria, genetic dispositions and weaknesses etc. But there is a deeper factor at work here, a spiritual factor. We are out of balance with our whole being. Something needs to purify, to change so we can grow as Soul. Dustin's experience is a dramatic illustration of this shift in awareness.

Our Spiritual Bodies

What do we need to realize? What do we need to discover about our nature that is hidden from us at present? Just like Dustin discovered, these answers are found within our spiritual bodies. These bodies form our aura, and house key aspects of our make-up. The physical body is one that we are familiar with. But we also have an Emotional Body (often referred to as the Astral Body). And we have a Causal Body (called by some a Karmic Body). In addition we also have a Mental Body or Mind Body. All these bodies are an integral part of our being and it is in these other bodies that we can often locate the source of our imbalances and disharmonies that can cause our state of being ill-at-ease.

These bodies correspond to spiritual planes, heavens (the term in Christianity) or parallel universes, (the reference used by scientists) and are listed here in order of vibration or spiritual purity from lowest to highest. The Astral/Emotional Body relates to the Astral Plane, the Causal/Karmic Body relates to the Causal Plane, and the Mental/Mind Body relates to the Mental Plane. The Etheric Plane relates to the Etheric Body, referred to by metaphysicians and psychologists as the subconscious mind. The Etheric Plane is part of the Mental Plane, and is the last frontier before entering the higher pure worlds/universes/heavens of Spirit starting with the Soul Plane.

The Emotional (Astral) Body

Our Astral Body is the dwelling place of our emotions. There are five key negative emotions that reside here that are a common source of disharmony and disease in the physical body:

Lust, an uncontrolled, unbalanced craving for foods, substances, persons, things;

Anger and its many milder forms including annoyance, irritation, being upset, and on the other end of the spectrum, outright anger, and rage;

Greed and several offshoots such as being miserly, stingy, and unsharing;

Vanity, pride and its other forms such as conceit and arrogance;

Undue attachment to things, people, ideas and beliefs.

The positive side of these unbalancing, negative, disease-causing passions are:

Discrimination (making right choices);

Forgiveness/Tolerance;

Contentment;

Humility;

Detachment.

Placing our attention on these positive virtues is one sure way to move past situations - roadblocks in our life.

The Causal Body

The Causal Body is next in vibration. The Causal Plane is the record storehouse for our past experiences, memories and karmic patterns as Soul on Earth, known by many as the Akashic records. Soul has had many lifetime experiences. Every thought, word and action is recorded; all of our wonderful experiences and all of our not so wonderful thoughts words and deeds too. Our responses to our challenges and trials today allow us to get it right this time around. Life has a way of re-testing us so that we can learn.

Eventually all of our thoughts, words and actions are balanced out. In other words our karma is burned off and we are much more conscious of the impact of our interactions with others. We are lighter, more enlightened beings: we are a purer vehicle for God's love, giving love to all life. When we act with love in our heart, some call this being a co-worker with God, spreading God's love to all. But until we approach this state we may have to solve some challenges, perhaps as illness, financial problems, relationship issues or problems in career etc. As I said previously, the healing principles in this book can also help you to solve challenges in all areas of your life in addition to your health.

Part of the process of discovering the root causes of ill health lie in the causal body. In other words, what we have caused in the past carries with it a lesson or lessons to help us purify as Soul in the present. This purification process is moving us forward in our spiritual growth helping us adopt positive qualities of character such as forgiveness, compassion, empathy, caring and many more. (For a comprehensive list, see the appendix at the back of this book.)

So far then, we have emotions that may not be serving us any more that are causing imbalances, and now we have just added karma.

The Mental Body

The next source of illness can come from our Mental Body or Mind Body. This body that is part of our make-up is the source of our thoughts, beliefs, attitudes, opinions and predispositions. These have been with us for a long time and undoubtedly been imprinted on us by our parents, our social groups, our governments and media and collected in our mind body today as an intricate assortment of patterns. The mind likes its grooves, its comfort zones, however some of these beliefs and patterns may no longer be serving us as Soul on our journey of purification. Yet thought patterns can be very difficult to not only discover, but also to change.

I used to hold a thought pattern around shopping for the things I needed. In the past I would apply logic and research to my search for the best deals and quality I could find. I discovered in recent years that solely relying on my analytical processes was beginning to fail me. No longer were my choices standing up to the test of time. I began to realize that I needed to do my research but then to set the search aside with a postulate to Spirit: please bring into my life the best product for me that is in harmony with my needs and those of the whole. In this way I was working more with Spirit to create harmony in my life and for those around me. One example has been the recent search for an upgraded vehicle. My mind was saying "fuel efficient small car" but I ended up with a pick-up truck when I turned the final selection over to Spirit and let my dreams and other signs guide me. After a year, I can now see the benefits the truck has provided, carrying loads for various errands for my wife's new venture as well as long distance travel comfort , driving to new assignments.

As far as illness goes, some of your thought patterns may no longer be appropriate to the consciousness Soul is adopting, and so may be causing a disharmony in the physical body. More on this later.

So all together we have a number of places to look, to explore when we are working to uncover the underlying sources of our health and other issues.

The part can never be well unless the whole is well.

Plato

Now let's take our quest for spiritual purification and balance into the emotional realm.

8

Emotional Toxins

All emotions are pure which gather you and lift you up; that emotion is impure which seizes only one side of your being and so distorts you.

Rainer Maria Rilke, Bohemian-Austrian Poet

Caroline's Emotional Liberation

Caroline is a yoga teacher and Reiki practitioner and viewed herself as a calm, balanced and peaceful individual. However, one day a few years ago she was about to learn there is always one more step in Soul's growth and purification; she found herself in excruciating pain with a sciatic nerve problem. As a yoga teacher this was a major challenge. She told me, "I was in pain all the time, had difficulty moving and I finally found I had to stop teaching. For two years I lived with the pain but I was on a search for the reason. I was doing everything I could do to deal with it. The pain was running down my leg and I could hardly walk. I was trying yoga to stretch it out, I was icing it, I was seeing a chiropractor, even taking aspirin to sleep at night, and I was trying to figure it out from a spiritual standpoint in my meditations. I was asking myself what was out-of-balance in my life. It was at this two-year point that I surrendered to God, and in that act of surrender I could feel the energy coming in. I went into a healing cycle after that.

Surrender Opens up New Discoveries

"I began to follow a cookie crumb trail and it led me to a book written by a medical doctor. The book said I had to talk to my sciatic nerve. The author said that in his experience with thousands of patients that eighty per cent of back pain is psychosomatic and involved emotions. Shortly thereafter I found myself at a friend's dinner party and ended up talking to a fellow from India, a Jain (Jainism is one of the oldest religions in the world). After about ten minutes of chit chat, he said to me: 'You have a lot of anger in you.' I was floored. I turned to my good friend and asked her, 'do I have anger in me?' She said, 'of course not. You are a wonderful person.' Nevertheless, he said he felt a lot of anger. I denied this judgement at first, but his comment stuck with me.

"After that experience, a yoga teacher friend suggested I see a man who did emotional release work. In our session, he asked a lot of questions, particularly about people in my life. He combined his questions with kinesiology (muscle testing) and it was showing I was testing weak for several people – the men in my life. That realization sent me down the road of forgiveness – forgiving the men and then forgiving myself for not standing in my truth.

"Within two days of that session, all the pain disappeared! I suddenly could walk normally. The pain has never come back. If I feel a twinge, I talk to my back saying; 'I'm not going to allow you to seize up on me again. I am going to deal with my emotions and not let them have an impact on my body.'

"Shortly after the healing, I was motivated to take a weekend course in New York on being more aware of my emotions. This course revealed for me that I had blocked emotions in my body; I had to learn about when I was blocking and stifling, and when an emotion was a negative one. In this pivotal weekend I learned to identify emotions and figure out a way to release them in a healthy way, giving love to myself and to my world.

Developing a Stronger Connection with Spirit

"Throughout this discovery process I felt my connection to Spirit was guiding me through a process of healing during my meditations, helping me move forward with my life, revealing to me what I needed to do to move forward pain-free. The process gave me a feeling of incredible love and I could also feel a lot of energy. When I truly surrendered that day, that's when everything speeded up. My healing came in three weeks and for me I had experienced a miracle.

"One of my most significant moments was when a stranger said, 'You are an angry person.' It was such an out-of-the-blue comment; it pushed me to go in a new direction. When he said it, it was highlighted. I felt that his words were illuminated with lights – that there was a message for me.

Taking it to a Higher Level

"I was initially doing everything I could think of to help myself such as yoga, chiropractic treatments and massage, but I needed to change the focus of my search to a higher level of exploration. I attribute a lot of my success solving this healing puzzle from doing Reiki II, absent healings on myself, and in the process I was writing down feelings and impressions which were helping me connect. When I did the absent healings, it connected me with my higher self for guidance. I was examining who I was.

"Most importantly, I had to have humility to change my self-beliefs. I thought of myself as this wonderful, kind, peaceful person but underneath all of this was anger. I needed spiritual help to see it. I had to look at myself as human and admit I had this anger; I wasn't this divine serene being I imagined I was. I had to admit I had some negative traits – I was not as loving and peaceful as I had thought. So I needed humility to get down on my knees to ask God for help.

"There was a huge shift in me!

Spiritual Realizations Flood In

"I've discovered a new level of compassion for others going through a human experience in this spiritual healing process. It's given me so much understanding for others and a huge love and respect for it. I feel such gratitude for this life where I can grow, learn and expand."

When I asked Caroline if she has discovered new spiritual principles operating in her life, she replied, "One I really recognized is that I have come here to be joy. I can see my purpose a lot clearer now. When I get out of harmony, out of balance, I lose consciousness of who I am and I am no longer fulfilling my purpose of being joy.

"I have also needed to learn detachment – detachment from the belief and image I had constructed of myself. I believed I was this peaceful being which was not true. I had to let go of this false image that I had created and believed to be true, accept who I truly am and to love myself. You see, my whole life was image (Caroline was an actor earlier in life). It wasn't real. I had to be authentic, honest and learn. I had to ask myself, 'what am I truly feeling?'"

What is Emotion?

The fact that man does not know himself becomes our search into healing. Our emotions are so much a part of us that we cannot see them in their true light. A part of our journey of purification in this lifetime is recognizing patterns of behaviour that are integral to our being and their consequent emotional components. Emotions that are no longer serving us are at the center of many disharmonies in our being and can be the cause of disease in their extreme manifestation.

Emotion is energy in motion (e-motion). It excites, stirs, and agitates our feelings and can either contribute to our upliftment or the degradation of our harmony. Our emotions can be beneficial like laughter, or counterproductive to our being like anger. Should we harbour an emotion for a period of time that runs counter to our overall constitution, an aberration can develop. Then there is a part of us that is not in harmony with the whole. The severity of the gap between our overall harmony or vibration and the feeling of disharmony, will determine our overall state of balance or imbalance.

Theses disharmonies have then found a place of residence in our bodies and can become visible as discomfort, illness, a condition or an abnormality. Some of the most common negative emotions that can affect us are fear, hate, sorrow or grief, and worry.

Walter Bowman Russell, a natural philosopher and known for his unified theory in physics and cosmology, stated that the universe was founded on a unifying principle of rhythmic balanced interchange and related this to our own worlds within our bodies as follows:

God thinks in balanced waves of light. His universal body is, therefore, in perfect balance. His entire universe does not vary in its balance by the weight of one electron. If there were the slightest variation in the balanced rhythms of God's thinking – for even one moment – countless millions of lives on millions of planets in starry systems of His body would be snuffed out instantly and millions of years would elapse before life would again be possible upon those planets because of that momentary unbalance. Terrific eruptions upon nebulae and suns would transform them into entirely different intensities.

Yet that is exactly what happens to a man's body when he becomes angry, or fearful, or hates another man. Our bodies are made up of countless miniature solar and starry systems exactly as God's body is similarly constructed. If we upset the balance of their rhythmic motion, the wave-patterns become distorted and erupt with a violence measured by the intensity of the unbalanced emotion. And that is not all, for an unbalanced and unrhythmic body is vulnerable to deadly microbes and other infections from which rhythmically balanced bodies are insulated.

Fear Shuts Out Love

The emotion of fear and the emotional anxiety it brings shuts out love, trust and creativity. It is a most destructive emotion that can stop Soul in its tracks from moving forward on its journey. Soul's destiny may want to take it into new situations, relationships, careers - activities for its growth and learning, but fear has the power to halt this progress. The result can be manifested as an internal conflict reflected in the body. This can make itself known as a minor condition at first but then become a full blown challenge.

Most "dis-ease" (disharmony) follows a pattern of progression. First the imbalance is known at higher levels, perhaps felt in the heart as a knowingness. But as this heart-feeling is ignored and the imbalance or desire to follow Soul's agenda is suppressed by a fear, the situation may then present itself as a conscious awareness or thought. Ignoring these thoughts then can translate into the physical body. Further suppression of the issue via medical or natural interventions may forestall the condition but there may be an eventual level of seriousness that manifests, Soul's way of getting us to listen to its message.

Many conditions can be brought under control by being aware of this process of manifestation of disharmonies. If something does not feel right, the disharmony can be corrected by making changes. So the body "talks" to us, and our emotions can be a key place to look for the source of the condition or for a piece of the puzzle.

One such outcome of fear is a lack of flexibility. This can reflect in the body as a stiff neck or sore or diseased joints as I have discovered on my own life-adventure. Today, whenever I feel stiffness in a joint or in my neck, I ask myself where my inflexibility is coming from. Or, how gracefully am I accepting a change?

"Whatever happens in our emotional body also occurs in our physical body...Through the mind-body connection, any repressed feelings of wanting and deserving harmony, peace, stability, and a

simple sense of joy in life are translated into appropriate bio-chemical responses in the body. This effectively deprives the body cells of all these positive qualities as well."

"Whatever you keep to yourself out of fear of being criticised or hurt, actually turns into poisons in the body."

Andreas Moritz, author of *Cancer is Not a Disease, It's a Survival Mechanism*

Love, the Antidote to Fear

The antidote to fear is love. Fear cannot exist where there is love. Embodied in love is confidence and trust. Soul wants to grow beyond the false limitations of fear. Our anxieties may be hidden in such things as resisting changes. We may feel we are comfortable where we are, but are we really resisting out of deeply embedded trepidation? We are being stretched beyond our comfort zone. An honest examination of one's self is required here, exploring the hidden aspects of our nature, something we may not want to open up. This may reveal a hidden fear of failure, or of loss, for example.

Often, Soul is ready for something new and is calling for a new setting for its growth, requiring a change in relationships, career, residence and more. Love in a spiritual sense is all about trusting that there is good in all change. The expression, "It's all good" sums this up succinctly.

But how does one conquer fear. First by recognizing that it is fear that is inhibiting your movement forward into the future. Second, by asking for help in conquering the fear and accepting the change. Third, by taking action.

Conquering Fear with HU

The most powerful tool I can offer is contemplation and singing HU or your own spiritual sound in combination with it. This has the ability to take one past the mind that is thinking about the situation and into the realm of Soul that is accepting of all experiences. Soul is love, and the gateway is through your heart. Open your heart to love and you can move out of fear.

Exercise: Letting Go

Sit comfortably in an easy chair, close your eyes and gently place your attention on the screen of your imagination, a point just above and between your eyebrows. Begin to quietly sing HU or your special personal word-sound either aloud, softly or silently to yourself. Look for spiritual light and also listen for inner sounds. After a few minutes, imagine yourself climbing a magnificent staircase that leads up into a blue sky dotted with white fluffy clouds. Take a few minutes to climb the staircase. Now see yourself walking through the clouds and into a realm of beautiful pale golden light. This is the Soul plane, the home of Soul. As you reach the top of the staircase, walk along a path in the beautiful light and study the nature around you. You feel lighter as you walk and you feel the warmth of the light purifying your being, washing away all thoughts of your situation. When you are ready to return, you notice a trash can at the top of the staircase. Deposit any left-over cares and concerns into the bin before you come back down to Earth. When you get to the bottom of the stairs, you feel lighter, free and loving, and feel like passing this loving feeling on to others with a smile or a helping hand.

Sorrow and Disharmony

The second of the emotional downfalls is sorrow or grief. Grief causes a serious negative disharmony in our being if left too long. We need to allow ourselves a reasonable amount of time to heal from any loss whether it is the loss of a loved one, the loss of a job or even the loss of our financial security. Healing from these losses can follow the five stages of grief and healing from loss that Elizabeth Kubler-Ross defined: denial, anger, bargaining, depression, and acceptance. The first four components of this process are a negative drain on our harmony and can occur in any order, can be revisited or be wrapped up in a package of grief. This grief, left unattended can sap your energy, shut down your heart keeping you from love, and this can manifest as disease. Sadness and feeling down are other negative aspects of this emotional state.

One of my greatest challenges in recent years was serving as a hospice volunteer, helping patients and their loved ones deal with anticipated loss and actual loss. One key learning I took away from my three years in this volunteer service was to empower patients and those close to them. In this process there seemed to be inherent in the experience a willingness to address feelings, to get them out into full expression. I could see that this was more helpful in moving through the loss than not acknowledging the feelings, hanging on to them, prolonging the grieving process.

Moving into Healing from Grief

With the help of others, you can come to know and feel that life is just, and that you can learn from your experience and move forward. In this process you gain strength as Soul to conquer all challenges. Through the process of loss you are learning empathy, surrender, acceptance, gratitude and many other qualities that Soul wishes to strengthen through this experience. As in tackling fear, contemplation can be a wonderful tool to use to connect you with Soul and your highest perspective, helping you heal from your loss in a genuine way.

Worry and Stress

If you are focussed on the past, you can tend to be regretful or remorseful. If your attention is on the future, you can feel worry which will result in stress. By this I mean that if your thoughts are dominated by what *may* happen, then you are creating a condition of worry and causing stress in your body. This emotion can be very damaging to your health over time. The key here is to recognize where you are. Do you lament the past, what could have been, what you could have done better? Are you thinking about what could happen or that something might not go well? The key is to find middle ground, the present moment.

If you are putting your attention in the past or future, perhaps you can find the present. It can be a very calm place. The future has not occurred, and the past can be forgotten, water over the dam so to speak. Try to find that present moment of contentment. Contemplation can help you to place your attention in the present moment and to fill your "present" with love.

To be in the present, you have to be in a position to enjoy every moment. If your life is a series of destinations connected by travel time in between, chances are you are rushing through life and giving yourself a great deal of disease-causing tension in the process. The key is to slow down and live the transition time as in-the-moment time. Slow your driving, slow your walking down, and leave more time to get places so you can relax - even plan on arriving early!

The Five Channels of Self-Destruction and Illness

We are on our own path of purification and this is occurring on several levels; this is a journey into higher vibrations that are linked to our changes in consciousness. Our harmonious make-up is a moving target as we grow in awareness, conscious realizations and elevate our vision of who we are. Our destiny is spiritual mastership and this physical lifetime has provided us with the setting to learn some key personal lessons.

These lessons center around five channels or behaviours that have a negative pole and a positive pole. The negative pole represents the lowest attributes of the human condition, and the opposite pole is our goal, spiritual perfection and mastership of the human condition. At the positive pole, we have reached a point of total service to all life and as a co-worker with the Creator, God, we are dedicated to helping others in their life journey.

These five channels of growth exist for everyone and, in this present moment, we each have our own place within these channels somewhere between the poles.

The five negative poles are defined as lust (self-indulgence), anger, greed, vanity and attachment.

The five positive poles are: discrimination (making right choices), forgiveness, contentment, humility and detachment.

Companion Emotions of the Five Channels

These five channels carry with them companion emotions that can be the source of illness and an opportunity for your purification. They represent a continuum for our growth and we find ourselves living in these channels as we go about our daily living. How we interact with others is the key, and by understanding these channels, we can see where our current position is and what may be underlying a state of dis-ease or illness. Our growth as Soul is tied directly to these five channels in the human condition. Because we are on this life-path of purification, these channels within us need to be purified and if one channel is out of step or balance with our total being or consciousness, it can cause illness. So in order to unravel a cause we must look inward, and honestly evaluate our position within these channels.

These channels have an influence on all of the bodies we carry: the physical, emotional, causal and mental. At this moment, let's take a look at the emotional body influences these channels hold, and our way of living within each as part of our voyage of discovery regarding possible root causes and potential areas of purification/healing.

Lust (Self-indulgence): Indulging One's Own Desires Without Restraint

Lust is having an abnormal appetite for drugs, alcohol, tobacco, highly spiced foods, fatty foods, sweets, highly processed snack foods and sex. Some manifestations in human behaviour are gluttony, reading obscene material, and self-gratification.

Other manifestations are an abnormal appetite for money, power, things, and recognition, and these imbalances may sow the seeds of disharmony in our body. This can show up in a person as being self-centered and uncaring of others. It places one at the low end of the scale of human evolution - the opposite pole being discrimination and balance - making right choices. Somewhere between these two poles you will find yourself.

Sooner or later, Soul will want to continue its movement toward the positive polarity and these behaviours, however mild will need purification. Taking another step forward will be necessary.

Exercise: Discovering Hidden Imbalances

Could there be an aspect of this Lust Channel that is no longer resonating with your total being? In other words, do you have a craving or a need that is a 'must have'? Here could be the source of an imbalance, as subtle as it may be, that needs your attention. Contemplate on your life as reflected in this channel to see where you are and what changes you may have to make, keeping in mind that you are not perfect, yet! What can you learn about yourself that could assist you as a piece of the puzzle in an overall healing? Review your life in terms of your need for drugs, alcohol, tobacco, money, power, things, foods and recognition.

Anger: My Way or the Highway

Anger stirs up trouble and represents an extreme position of, "I want it my way." Anger says, "This is not what I want," and, "I'm not flexible." It is resistance to the way things have unfolded. So as such, anger is an extreme form of resistance to the flow of life and could be a major source of imbalance.

Anger creates hatred and causes emotional burn-out. Jealously, malice and resentment are companion negative emotions that are fuelled by anger, one's resistance to the way life is unfolding at that time. Milder forms of anger include annoyance, brooding, irritation, being ticked-off, agitation and impatience.

Being dismissive with another person, their ideas or their behaviours, or, anger at a situation that may feel like a loss of face, has a habit of affecting the angry one profoundly. Other behavioural aspects of anger include slander, gossip, profanity, faultfinding, peevishness, mockery and ill will.

Anger is an impediment to contemplation and meditation and clouds the mind, and it is usually expressed in a harsh way which destroys relationships. (Anger can also be expressed as a simmering silence.)

All anger, even in its milder forms has the potential to manifest as illness, and uncontrolled anger over a period of time can manifest as deep-seated disease. (Reflect back on Caroline's issue with her sciatic nerve.) Some say that depression is anger turned inward. Others link Cancer to anger and describe Cancer like a war going on in the body, a struggle between what the mind wants and what the heart is seeking. As indicated above, anger can take some very mild forms so you need to be aware of these aspects that may need to change at your stage of growth and development as a Soul on a lifetime cleansing program.

The polar opposite of anger in this channel is forgiveness and tolerance. This is a key area for examination in your life. When something occurs in your life that has the potential to cause you anger or one of the milder forms of it such as irritation, frustration or annoyance, the faster you can rebalance into forgiveness or tolerance, the better off you are.

Exercise: Key Questions on Anger

Where do you fit on this scale between anger and forgiveness?

Are you impatient? Can you easily modify your expectations of yourself and others?

Do you get even mildly irritated at times?

How quick are you to forgive another or yourself?

Who can you forgive in your life right now?

Do you participate in gossip, profanity or faultfinding?

What can you let go of in order to move forward in your life?

Are you able to easily listen to the viewpoint of others without having to share yours?

Greed and its Many Forms

Greed fixes us to the materialistic things of life such as money and its surrogates. It is an extreme focus on attaining and maintaining wealth. It shows its ugly face as miserliness, being stingy, a lack of sharing, deception and trickery.

Subtle forms of greed can manifest as fibs, distortions and "little white lies" which usually have the goal of getting something at the expense of another. It often can involve emotional manipulation and emotional blackmail.

The positive polarity is being content with one's life and financial condition. Know that we have earned our condition in life through our past behaviors, and that in this life we need to see that everything we have must be earned either through work, service or by being paid for. There is no fast track through greed to wealth, as this self-destructive behavior will eventually result in an unbalancing in the physical body or at some other level in our being.

The Polar Opposite of Greed is Contentment.

Are you content with your life, within your own skin?

Are you happy to share what you have?

Do you give freely of yourself?

It is difficult to see the many manifestations of greed that could be a part of our character, being immersed in this Western society. The best way to take an objective viewpoint is to look at your ability to give freely, serving others.

How sharing are you?

Do you give freely with no strings attached, or do you attach an expectation of reciprocity to your giving, or an expectation of love or friendship?

Exercise on Generosity:

Where do you see yourself in this channel and where is there room for change in moving closer to the positive pole, contentment, serving/helping others? Examine yourself in light of the questions in the two paragraphs above.

Vanity Has its Disguises

Vanity at the emotional level manifests as egotism, the overgrown opinion of one's self. Behavioural manifestations are arrogance, haughtiness or pride. Vain people can be quite sensitive to criticism. Being a control freak is another hallmark of vanity or pride.

This negative channel that we find ourselves within can also manifest with us in an excessive focus on our physical appearance, pride or a preoccupation with how we think others see us. Some manifestations could be over attention given to position, title, cars we drive, clothing we wear and our neighbourhood, or size of house. Some of the behaviours that flow from vanity are bragging, faultfinding and scolding, pride and haughtiness. Vanity in its extreme form has an expression in the need to punish those who oppose us.

Remember that you are a unique being and at this stage in your spiritual growth, these aspects of vanity may be very subtle. The key words here are "over attention."

Vanity can also take the form of "spiritual vanity", in this case letting the emotions or thoughts and beliefs rule over the heart, the gateway to Soul. When the emotions and thoughts rule, we close off our heartfelt desires, our true inner nature as Soul. Spiritual vanity ignores the whisperings of Soul in favour of reactions that feed the ego, the material being. By this I mean that you may not be following your spiritual nudges, intuitions or other forms of guidance, or you are not maintaining your spiritual connection through contemplation. In other words you may be underutilizing your spiritual connection by getting caught up in your emotions or your thoughts, and this is also a form of vanity.

This arrogance can be destructive to one's overall harmony and manifest as being ill-at-ease in some way. I have discovered for me, this connection between Soul and the lower self is represented by the knee, which is my symbolic connection between the higher and lower self. When I have a knee problem, it reflects to me a need to connect better with Soul by listening to my heart.

The Attributes of Humility

Humility is the polar opposite quality we strive for as conscious beings on the road of life, the journey of purification. Examples of humility include:

Modesty, a desire to not seek credit;

A willingness to listen to others without a need to share our views;

Not having to be right or convince others of our position or our truth;

Wanting to serve or help others on their terms and to be yielding.

Exercise on Vanity and Humility

Take a look at your place in this channel between Vanity and Humility from this point-of-view by asking yourself:

When faced with opposition to your ideas or proposals, how humble are you? How open are you to the ideas of others? How respectful are you of others?

> Are appearances important to you? Do you feel a need to impress others with the things of life like cars, clothing and houses?
>
> Where are your opportunities for spiritual growth and bringing about a new harmony in your being?

Attachment Offers One More Opportunity for Growth

As with all things in spiritual growth, there is always one more step on the path toward mastership of our lessons. This channel of self destruction and illness involves the *unnecessary* attachment to anything in this materialistic world, as well as to emotions, thought patterns and beliefs.

Attachment fixes us to the lower values of life including our surroundings, associations and relationships with others. It involves placing false values on the trappings of life such as home, position, possessions, vehicle one drives etc. and leads to emotional conditions like worry and anxiety. They say the top worry of wealthy people is the loss of money. Fear of loss rears its head again!

Attachment can also be present in rigidity of thoughts and beliefs, representing inflexibilities which can inhibit our growth. I grew up with the belief that money came from work. In recent years I have had to let go of that belief and recognize that money can come from investments that have unexpected returns which have manifested because I have developed new levels of trust in my inner guidance. Money can come in the form of gifts as well.

Contentment with our life, our families, our things – what we own - is the polar opposite of attachment. This is a consciousness of knowing that everything we have is for our growth as Soul. The things of life are but props that are to be moved on and off our stage of life to allow us to move through different scenes that are set for our learning. Holding on to our current stage setting can have the effect of stifling Soul's growth.

How easily do you let go of the things in your life, emotions and thought patterns that may no longer be serving your best interests?

Ask Yourself....

Are you hanging on to relationships, social positions, or a job?

Do you consider that the things you have are on loan from Spirit?

Do you understand that to receive something new into your life, you have to make room for it by letting go of other things that are no longer needed?

How easily can you let go of unnecessary things and move on?

What is the degree of clutter in your home, office or life in general? There is a relationship between all these areas, and clutter in one area can affect the free flowing energy in another area of your life.

Finding Balance through Detachment

The opposite pole on the Attachment scale is Detachment, a state of being non-attached to things, people, honours, position, residence and more. It is a state of allowing these physical attributes to flow through our lives as stage decorations or props for our current lesson plan and the people we are meant to interact with and learn from in a spiritual sense. The easier we can flow through situations and their physical elements, the more we can grow and purify, and heal in the process.

Detachment also implies flexibility, being open to new ideas and a having a willingness to make changes outside our comfort zone.

Exercise: Uncovering Areas of Attachment

How do you define yourself? By your position, job, marriage partner, your home and furnishings? Or do you define yourself by your values, the qualities present in your life.

How do you relate to others? Is the first question you ask another on meeting for the first time: "What do you do?" or, "Where do you live?" Or do you want to get to know the individual as a person?

All of these subtleties are clues to your self-assessment of your current place in the Attachment-Detachment Channel and where the possibilities for spiritual healing/growth lay. How can you move forward into a life of greater spiritual harmony?

Making Emotional Changes

This chapter on searching the emotional body has only provided some ideas on the effects of emotions on your physical body and where to look for the causes of your illness or where healing is needed. Looking at our very nature is not easy. It will involve a process over time of peeling back the layers. To get you started with an honest examination of where you can move forward in your emotional make-up, try the following self-evaluation exercise.

Exercise: Evaluating Your Emotional Next Steps

On each line, fill in a step you can take into greater harmony along your path to healing.

Negative Pole	**Step(s) I can take** **Positive Pole**
Fear	**Love**
Fears in my life	Love in my Life
Holding back	Adventurous
Doubts, Reticence	Confidence
Grief and Sorrow	**Happiness and Joy**
Sadness, Feeling Down, Depression	Enthusiasm for Life
Dealing with grief	Feeling Love of Spirit
Lust	**Discrimination**
Seeking Power and Authority	Serving Others

Self-centered	Caring
Anger	**Forgiveness**
Irritation, Dismissive	Respect
Impatience	Tolerance
Greed	**Contentment**
Stingy, Miserly	Giving Without Conditions
Deceptions, Fibs, Little White Lies	Truthful, Open, Honest
Emotional Manipulation	Purity, Kindness
Vanity	**Humility**
Ego, Arrogance	Empowering Others
Control Freak	Relaxed, Creative
Spiritual Vanity	Following Your Heart
Attachment	**Detachment**
Worry, Anxiety	Letting go, finding center
Jealously	Acceptance
Defined by People, Position, Possessions	Defined by interests, values Service to others

The secret of health for both mind and body is not to mourn for the past, not to worry about the future, or not to anticipate troubles, but to live the present moment wisely and earnestly.

Buddha 563-483 BC

Now let's take our journey of spiritual healing into the causal realm, the world of cause and effect (karma).

9

Uncovering Past Karma to Heal the Present

The game of life is the game of boomerangs. Our thoughts, deeds, and words return to us sooner or later, with astounding accuracy.
Florence Scovel Shinn, New Thought spiritual teacher

Anastasia's Lifelong Purification

Anastasia has been living with back pain, what she calls her "rotten back" for over sixty years. She was working at age seventeen when she twisted it, and since that time has been living with back pain on and off all her life. "It's been more on than off," she told me, "and I've been seeing chiropractors for years."

In 1987 I even saw a Shaman. He went into contemplation, and when he came out he told me he could take the edge off it, but nothing more. Over the years, Anastasia told me, "When I have to do something, make a change in life, and when I resist, my back goes out. Then I need to see a chiropractor. For example, when I needed to leave the big city to help my mom in a town a few hours away, I resisted and got a bad back again. When I needed to move again, and resisted, I fell and broke my hip! This is a pattern of not listening and not following through, not catching on to what I need to do," she told me.

Contemplations Lead to Acceptance

Anastasia continued: "Through daily contemplations, morning and before bedtime, I have grown into a kind of acceptance. This acceptance has been aided by about fifteen powerful and clear dreams that have given me a look at past lives where this bad back issue all began. These experiences were so very clear and I knew it was me doing these terrible things – Oh my God! I needed to see them and accept their realities. And so certain people were in my life this time again.

"This has been a real gift. I can see the causes of my bad back now – karma. Looking back in this present life I know where I've gone wrong. I've seen in these dreams where I was a victim, but, I can extrapolate now what I did as the cause factors. In many of these lives, I was with people I've met and interacted with in this life. I now know what I did and the results of my past actions. I've learned a few things - like I need to learn to listen.

"I've tried to have inner talks with my spiritual guide, but I'm not getting much – I have a strong feeling I have to live with this condition. In other words, I need to pay off this karma. After sixty years, I've come to a point of acceptance now that I need to go through it. I'm not sure if I should be looking for a healing because it won't fix the cause which I earned. I need to wear it.

I know I'm Protected

"Looking back on my life, I can see that I've been protected. I've been prevented from doing stupid things, and kept out of harm's way. For example, one night I was volunteering and a friend came in and talked to me way past closing time, delaying my normal time of departure. On the way home I passed two serious accidents within two blocks. I just knew I was protected from that experience. Also

I've had pneumonia eight times. On one occasion I was out for four days, it was so serious. So I'm being protected and I also know that there is no way I'm going to get out of this life until I'm done, until I've burned off my karma. So I get help when I need it, but I also need to pay. All in all, I've had a good life in spite of this awful back, so I just need to find the balance.

"I've come to the realization that in past lives, anything I've put down on paper has caused issues for me, so today, my inner overriding voice says, 'don't reveal your secrets,' so I don't use a diary. This way I can't read it over again. I know that I need to let go of the past, not remember it. I feel like I'm living by the seat of my pants, yet I do a lot of internal talking with my spiritual guide. I live alone so I mirror myself. This gives me answers.

Moving Away from Anger

"I've had a temper all my life, but I could control it if the circumstances were not terribly personal. Today, I've come along way. I let it be, now. I see others as just what they are, Souls with a lot to learn. This makes it easier to let go of situations and to let the anger go with it.

"I know I can't fight my back situation. I just go to the chiropractor if I need to. It gets fixed for a week or so. I know I have to go through a number of things at this point. Right now it's so bad I can hardly walk and I'm using a walker instead of a cane. I know I have to see a surgeon about surgery. It's that or a nursing home.

"But my constitution is strong after thirty-five years on my spiritual journey. It's been my spiritual teaching that has kept me on my feet, learning to cope with the pain. I don't say: 'Why me?' It's fine if this is the way it works. I know whatever happens, happens for a reason. And I've learned a few things along the way, particularly about karma. After all these years, there has had to be some cleansing going on with me. I've seen fifteen past lives but there is much more to clean up. My past life dream experiences connected me to people I've met in this life such as my father and other relationships. I've met one person in this life that I was married to several times in the past, but I was forced into it by my father on those occasions. I hope I've said good bye to those sets of circumstances now.

Detachment, another Key

"Key for me in my spiritual growth in this life has been learning more about detachment. Some things bothered me for years, and if I can say no to these things – to let go – I'm better off. These things include stuff and people I need let be. They have to live their life. So I'm detaching myself from things that don't mean anything anymore. When you see the past so clearly, you know it's a fact. I needed to come into agreement with it, acknowledge it and let it go. Memories are not good for me. I need to let it go and focus on the present.

"For me, my dreams reinforced the reality of reincarnation and that things from the past have to be dealt with. Some people don't see this, and repeat it over and over again. I want to finish it off, whatever I can, not incurring any more karma in these relationships forever."

~

Karma – Why We are Here

Karma is the main reason why we are where we are. It is the cause of our current family setting, other relationships, friends, work, country, financial circumstances, genetic predispositions, personal preferences, character and wellness. These components of our life are a precisely constructed lesson package.

The set of circumstances we call our life is a bundle of karma that has been shaped by our past thoughts, words and actions. These karmic influences come from our past lives as Soul, and this present lifetime as well, and attract us to people, places and things, all for our greater unfoldment. As an example, falling in love is really falling into karma - i.e. a karmic attraction. The issues that need the most attention are brought to us in our closest relationships - spouses, family, friends and work associates. We are attracted to these people, conditions and situations which can also be referred to as karmic attraction.

Our karma has been earned and what we call the good in our lives can be attributed to our good acts of previous times. And the so called bad in our lives, our challenges, can be traced to our past as well, areas of needed growth for Soul. Karma is usually rebalanced and resolved through three avenues: financial, service and pain. Of the three, it seems that pain and discomfort move us forward the most and reshape us into a better version of who we are as Soul.

Disharmonies occur in our bodies for our purification from outmoded physical, mental, and emotional habits, and patterns from our past. As discussed before, these disharmonies can manifest in the body as discomfort, chronic conditions, illness, disease and even accidents and injury.

An integral part of the healing process is taking responsibility, and so as karma can be part of our current healing puzzle, we need to add it to our search for causes and also include it in the process of regaining balance and harmony – our well-being. Karmic patterns can be the sole cause of an imbalance or simply a part of it.

A Path to Resolving Karma

First, as part of our personal search for truth and rebalancing, we need to understand that karma is playing a primary role in our current overall set of conditions and is the reason why we have incarnated on Earth. If we had no karma, there would be no need for being here. Our growth would be finished here in this big schoolhouse and we would be graduated to a "college" or "university" for Soul's greater purification in a higher realm, another spiritual plane or heaven. So everyone has karma to recognize, deal with and learn from.

Second, one needs to take responsibility for it. At this point you may not understand what it is, but you need to be willing to accept that if there is a problem, karma could be involved in some way. This means you are open to seeking the underlying cause or causes that were set in motion in the past and to make changes in rebalancing these conditions emanating from the past.

Third, you need to take action to seek out the cause(s). You will be given some tools and references later in this chapter, but suffice it to say that you need to be an active participant in this process. You need to be creative and become the explorer.

Fourth, you will need to be prepared to accept the conscious realizations when you uncover them or when they are revealed to you. Like Anastasia, there is the possibility that you were quite an awful person in a past setting, and you need to be able to see this, accept it for what it was, and then see how it fits with your present circumstances. This situation may also represent a chain of events stringing out over several lifetimes.

A Frozen Shoulder

When searching for the cause of my frozen shoulder one day in contemplation, I discovered that part of the issue was seated in the past. I was able to see that I had speared another in the shoulder in battle, but they had done the same to me in the previous lifetime, and then this pattern had its roots in a lifetime before that.

There is no simple one-time occurrence in most of these situations. There is most likely a karmic chain that needs to be recognized and worked out. In addition to physical acts, these karmic chains also involve the words, thought patterns, beliefs, and emotions that were, and now are, part of the event(s). With regard to the frozen shoulder, I asked for forgiveness and I forgave the other individual (Soul), as an acknowledgement of the past. This freed me up to look at a present day pattern I also needed to let go of which had me "frozen" in a career project as opposed to me being more flexible.

Fifth, you need to find ways to resolve the pattern that is no longer serving you. At this juncture there are some big keys to moving forward; acceptance of the truth about your past, and forgiveness and apologizing to those you hurt (remember Caroline from chapter 8). This process is about changing. It involves shifting to a new space, a new consciousness of being.

Changes of any magnitude seem to only work with major incentives whether they are negative or positive, to move out of our physical, emotional and mental comfort zones. Tilting the scales from greed to giving, from anger to forgiveness, from ego to humility or from lying and cheating to total honesty can be a lifetime project for Soul, or can occur in a moment, an epiphany. Some people have lifetimes filled with change and progress, and others seem to have very predictable linear lifetimes, growing in a very stable setting or set of conditions. Again, the caution here is not to judge your life by what you see in others.

Healing from Past Life influences

As with examining the physical and emotional bodies, like Anastaisia, you need to be the active participant in designing your own path to wholeness when it comes to resolving karmic issues.

Contemplation or meditation in the form of creative visualization is key, and in combination with singing HU or another spiritually charged sound, both together can work wonders to help you resolve your karma. In contemplation you can see yourself in a detached way on the stage of life and previously invisible patterns can be made visible. Make this a regular good habit, a part of your day that you dedicate to yourself and the changes that you would like to happen, the healing you would like to experience in your life.

Never be afraid to sit awhile and think.

Lorraine Hansberry, Author of *A Raisin in the Sun*

> **Exercise: Addressing Personal Karma**
>
> If your challenge(s) involve another person(s), go into contemplation singing HU or other spiritually charged sound. After a while, visualize meeting the person as Soul. Be kind and open with the person and have a conversation with them. Start with pleasantries and then move the conversation to the subject of your problems. Explain your side, then listen for them to explain their viewpoint.
>
> Be open. Don't judge them. Ask them how you can heal the situation and move forward.
>
> This technique can have dramatic results and open your eyes to another viewpoint.

I once had a boss that would come and sit in my office for over an hour every day, just chatting. I could not get my work done and during the conversation he would ask me to do several more projects, an impossible workload. I was really feeling the *stress*! There was no way he would respond to my request to let up and give me space, so I took the challenge into contemplation. I chatted with him Soul to Soul and explained how I felt, how stressed he was making me feel. The next day, everything shifted. From that day on, he would pass my office and say hello, but he never came in for a long conversation again. This was a dramatic experience for me — solving a challenge at a higher spiritual level.

Eight Keys to Resolving Karma

1 **Asking for help:** Ask Spirit or your spiritual guide to help you see what past thoughts words and deeds may be playing a part in your present situation.

2   Listen and look for answers: These may come in the form of dreams, Waking Dreams or Signs, Golden-tongued Wisdom (audio signs), a book or story, a flash of insight and any of the other ways Spirit can assist you as presented earlier.

3   Service to others: Selfless giving is another key to successfully unravelling a challenge. This takes the attention off the self and places it outward on others. It has the effect of opening the heart which is the gateway to Soul and to Spirit. With a genuinely open heart, the love of God enters and has an opportunity to impress upon your being the steps you need to take to healing. This may include a conscious realization of what needs to change within you. It could also provide you with a direct perception of the past circumstances and behaviours that set your present life conditions in motion so that you can begin to make changes. It could also open you up to greater receptivity and to new alternatives you have never considered before.

4   Charity: Generosity also opens the heart. Being generous with your time, talents and money is a great way to make changes in your life and well-being. Start with what you can and go from there. Limited finances, poor mobility or a perceived lack of skill or knowledge are just forms of procrastination. Volunteering can be a large part of your charity adventure into giving. We all have opportunities to be charitable and this represents a polar opposite move forward, away from many limiting traits that we are leaving behind as we expand in consciousness.

Some of my greatest realizations and leaps forward have occurred when I was volunteering intensively for several days at spiritual seminars. I'd paid my seminar fee but volunteered for much of the event, yet the service I gave had the effect of opening my heart to more love, creating a greater receptivity to what I needed in order to spiritually heal and move forward.

5   Giving Love: In this context, I am talking about spiritual love. Love has many faces. For you it could mean to bring joy into the lives of others by being cheerful. Or it may be by being humorous, bringing lightness to the lives of those around you. In other ways, one can be a good listener or interact with others with a new level of respect for their ideas and beliefs by reinforcing the choices they make as opposed to commenting with your opinion. This openness has a way of reflecting inward too, helping you open up to new healing possibilities and messages from the heart that can reveal solutions to past causes.

I've found in my life, the more resistance I have to a concept, the more I should do it. The resistance points at an obvious area where I need to make changes. It was for this reason that I became a hospice volunteer, which was a fantastic experience but very challenging for me. At the time I was very uncomfortable with the idea of death and the process of dying. After serving palliative patients in ways that I could in the hospital, in patient homes and at a hospice house, I developed a new level of comfort in discussing all kinds of issues ranging from the practical, to the emotional and spiritual. The greatest learning for me was to accept people the way they were, not to judge, and to help them on their terms, empowering them in the last days of their life.

6 **Silent Acts of Service**: This process of silently giving love will positively change you! Find one thing you can do each day for someone else without seeking any recognition or thanks. Do it quietly and discretely.

7 **Being Grateful**: You would be amazed at how this can change your life. Begin to appreciate the wonderful people, things and circumstances of your life. This creates a positive, can-do attitude and results in a major shift in energy. It turns a negative downward spiral into a positive uplifting spiral. I suggest a daily journal entry at the end of your day that simply says, I am grateful for (a person, friends, gifts from spirit, money, work, home, new realization etc.) today. Don't be afraid to share your appreciation of others with them and build them up too. Everyone loves to be appreciated!

8 **Journaling:** This can be very therapeutic and open up channels of insight and intuition you never thought possible. Remember, if you are feeling resistant to this idea, you should really do it! By recording my dreams, spiritual experiences and the events of my life, I have found I am better able to make connections and receive guidance that can help me solve problems big and small, steer clear of pitfalls plus avoid making costly mistakes. One technique is writing a letter to God. It is also a wonderful way to express your feelings and order your thoughts.

Journaling also has the benefit of allowing your thoughts to free-flow and the answers you seek can pour out onto the page. I have a monthly practice of writing a letter to Spirit in my journal summarizing the past months spiritual events, dreams, Waking Dreams/Signs, things going on in my life at the time etc. On one occasion, I made a note of something that was happening to my left ear. It felt like there was water in it at some times but not others. When I stood back and looked at all of my journal entries, there was a clear message that stood out. I wasn't listening to a particular important inner message. As soon as I changed course, the problem in the inner ear receded, then disappeared.

We can move past our karma but it does take an effort on our part. You have to be willing to explore and make changes, and reinvent yourself in the process.

Exercise: Exploring Past Lives to Heal Present Circumstances

In contemplation (singing HU or another spiritually charged word if you like) ask to be shown an event and time that is relevant to your current situation. Continue your contemplation and chanting aloud or silently for a while. After a few minutes, look into the screen of your imagination, your spiritual eye. Watch for light and listen for spiritual sounds. As the experience progresses, you may begin to imagine something that is relating to your question at the beginning of the exercise. Don't ignore it, go with it. When finished your contemplation, make an entry in your journal about the experience. Remember that you may be able to tie this experience to others in your dreams and everyday life that reveal the answers you need, although perhaps not what you're expecting. Expect the unexpected!

Exercise: Forgiveness

In contemplation, think of all the people that have hurt you in some way. Make a list in your mind. Now, forgive each one in turn. Let it all go. Let bygones be bygones. See yourself in a room filled with light from the windows. Walk toward the door, and go outside into the full sunlight and let it flood your body with warmth. A gentle warm breeze blows through your hair, carrying away with it all of life's hurts.

Exercise: Apologizing

In contemplation, make a mental list of the key people you may have hurt in your life. After a few minutes, one by one, apologize to each with a full explanation of the wrong you did and how sorry you are for the hurt you caused. Be sincere in your wish to heal the rift, to heal the past. Then after you have apologised to everyone on your list, imagine you are on a beach. Now get up from your beach towel and walk into the warm water and feel the cleansing, purifying effects of the water rebalancing your body at all levels. When you get out of the water you have a powerful feeling of being lighter and free.

Healing yourself is connected to healing others.

Yoko Ono, Artist, Musician, Author

A Mystery Issue

Karen found herself in a condition without explanation, a severely impaired neck and shoulder. She was in tremendous pain with seemingly no cause. The condition just showed up one day. She tried her regular doctor who prescribed pain medicine and muscle relaxants. These worked a little for a day or two but she was still off work, quite paralyzed by the condition.

The next week she was in to see her doctor for another visit and he admitted he was stumped about her condition. He could not find anything that could be the visible cause or trigger. He gave her a reference to a specialist in the local hospital, but also advised that because this specialist was the best in the country, he was in great demand and that it may take months to be able to see him. She left feeling quite bewildered but on arriving home, called to set up an appointment. Her doctor had already called to make the referral but the specialist's assistant did not seem optimistic about an early visit.

Shortly thereafter, she got a call back. Could she come in tomorrow? This was astonishing but what was even more amazing was that when she met the doctor, they realized they knew each other. They used to work together years ago when he was putting himself through medical school.

Within a few days of the visit and his treatment, she was back to normal! In a subsequent contemplation she realized there was some lingering karma between them that needed to be smoothed over. Her neck and shoulder condition was a gift from Spirit to bring her together with the specialist once again in this lifetime to resolve the issue forever.

12 Karma-Resolving Exercises and Actions

Here is a point form review to help you discover and resolve illness that may contain karmic roots:

1) Is there someone you need to meet Soul to Soul to resolve an issue?
2) Ask for help.
3) Listen and look for answers. Cultivate receptivity.
4) Service to others – helpfulness, listening, openness, non-judging.
5) Charity and generosity with your time, talents and money.
6) Give love by lifting up others with cheerfulness, humor and respect.

7) Silent acts of service/kindness.
8) Gratefulness daily exercise to open your heart and receptivity.
9) Journaling – opening up the channels of insight and intuition.
10) Do a contemplation to explore a past life or lives or gain insights.
11) Forgiveness of the past.
12) Apologizing for the past.

What is ill health? It's the result of a deliberate or else an unconscious violation of laws for a period of time. This ignorance of karmic law reflects imperfection. Healing then means doing something in a new way to regain health.

Harold Klemp,

Author of *A Modern Prophet Answers Your Key Questions about Life, Book 2*

Now let's take our exploration into the Mind Body arena.

10

Do Your Thoughts Pollute or Purify Your Body?

It is hard to let old beliefs go. They are familiar. We are comfortable with them and have spent years building systems and developing habits that depend on them. Like a man who has worn eyeglasses so long that he forgets he has them on, we forget that the world looks to us the way it does because we have become used to seeing it that way through a particular set of lenses. Today, however, we need new lenses. And we need to throw the old ones away.

Kenichi Ohmae, Business and Corporate Strategist, McKinsey and Company

Veronica's Realizations

Veronica has suffered from a stiff neck for about fifteen years. She told me that it is at the level of an annoyance, an inconvenience in her life, yet she also added that she knows that it's trying to teach her something.

When I chatted with her about this, she described her stiffness as moving from her neck up into the skull from her upper trapezius muscles and that her degree of discomfort related to her physical activities such as golf and other sports. She added that she has learned how to manage the discomfort through massage techniques. She felt that it was a condition she was "living with."

Uncovering Limiting Beliefs

In our conversation as we delved a little deeper into the issue she felt that her neck was representative of inflexibility to some degree in her attitude, perhaps reflecting limiting beliefs about her abilities and her career. She volunteered: "Maybe I'm not trusting, having faith in myself – faith in surrendering and moving forward with growing my business. It feels like I'm sitting on the fence," she revealed. "I want to bring abundance into my life. I know I can earn good money but I feel like I'm sitting on the fence in a comfortable position in not venturing out, not taking any risks." She added: "My concern is what my life will look like if I take a risk? I'm afraid I'll not have enough spare time." Fear seemed to be holding her back.

When I asked her about other insights she may have had, she shared a dream that has stayed with her for some time. In the dream which she feels was a scene from a past life, she was a man with a lot of power. She recalled: "He (I) would travel around from village to village with a cadre for supporters cutting off heads for really no reason. As he did this he felt proud and powerful, garnering support from his supporters." She feels that in this life she is experiencing neck issues to burn off karma from this past. But she began to connect some dots in our conversation; that having power in business in this life is related to her miss-use of power in the past.

Today she feels that she doesn't want to go down that road again for fear of appearing too powerful. Perhaps a fear of miss-using her power is at the core of this neck issue too?

Acknowledging Her Own Beliefs

Then something else flowed out, a belief that needs rebalancing. She told me that she is letting the opinions of others dictate her behaviors and aspirations. She shared with me that her boss talks negatively of other women who are successful, who are too wealthy, and that she is letting these opinions define her beliefs too. "I feel badly if I make money (I'm an independent contractor) and the boss knows about it. I'm letting it dictate how well I do. I realize now that her opinion is none of my business – I need to let go of this."

When we circled back to her fear of not having spare time, she realized that when she is working on her new business, she feels joyful. It is not eating up her free time. "It is how I want to spend my time!" she confessed.

Veronica realized that she needs to detach from the outcome of her work. She told me that she needs to build the foundation then add one layer on top of another without the expectation of what the outcome will look like.

She realized her stiff neck is teaching her three key lessons:

"First, I need to let go of the notions of allowing another's attitudes and opinions affect me and my abundance.

"Second, I don't have to be afraid of losing my free time as long as I'm doing what I love to do and I am joyful about it and not feeling resentful.

"Third, there is a karmic part of this too – I want to be financially successful without letting my ego take over. The power issue seems to be about being mouse-like versus being humble. I need to find a new balance and be able to speak up for myself.

Exploring Thoughts, Beliefs and Attitudes

The challenges we face in life including the areas of relationships, finances, work, and health are all opportunities for our greater unfoldment as Soul. What is most important for our lesson plan in this lifetime is how we deal with our difficulties as much as the solution. It's a combination of the process plus the end result.

We have discussed the emotional components to solving illness issues, our karma, what we set in motion in the past, and now we can explore our mental realm. This includes the effects our thoughts, beliefs, attitudes and predispositions can have on our well-being.

Changing Our Thought Patterns

Our thoughts and beliefs are such a part of us that we usually can't see how these Mental Body patterns can affect our health and wellness. But there can be a direct relationship. A thought pattern that we have grown up with may no longer be serving our growth as Soul. We may be too rigid in our beliefs and Soul needs us to open up to new ideas and possibilities as part of our journey. Maybe we need to tackle our challenges in a different way that is calling for a change in how we think, what we believe, and our attitude toward something. Perhaps we are not charitable and we need to learn to be more giving. For example, a present attitude of not giving hand-outs to beggars may have to change to learn this lesson about charity. I had this experience about ten years ago when I felt the urge to assist street people on my daily inner city walks. One day I even took a man shopping for lunch at small local grocers and shops so he could see how to buy the most nutrition with a small amount of money. I bought a carton of milk, some bananas and a big piled-high sandwich on a long bun at a deli, all for around four dollars. He even had some food left over for later. By assisting people on the edge through my small cash gifts and personal chats, I could see that I was becoming more compassionate, more open to life and less closed off to the circumstances of others.

Perhaps we need to be more open to spirituality in our life and so our current focus on the material things of life needs to shift. Or possibly one needs to see the challenges of others in a new light, and a greater empathy and respect is being called for by Soul. Our attitudes need to shift, moderate, or purify as we make progress on our personal path of spiritual enlightenment.

The key is seeing where the shift is required, uncovering the mind-body piece of the puzzle that is a part of the direct cause of our imbalance.

If in the last few years you haven't discarded a major opinion or acquired a new one, check your pulse. You may be dead.
Gelett Burgess, Author and Humorist

A Prostate Problem Rooted in the Mind

A number of years ago I began to have prostate issues. These were mild at first and so an herbal vitamin seemed to help for a while. But I was noticing that as time went on, the soreness was becoming hard to ignore. The vitamins were not doing their job and I knew that I had to do something. Seeing a doctor was my last resort because I knew in my heart that there was a message in this challenge, and other illnesses had taught me that I could not simply mask the symptoms with medications or surgery. I had to heal this situation at its root cause.

My first approach was contemplation and I began to put this issue front and center in my daily practice. And what came to me was to also ask for help in understanding the true source of this problem. What did I need to realize about myself? What did I need to change? What did I need to discover? What was my next step?

Well the answers came but not in the form that I expected! I had decided to attend a world-wide spiritual seminar that year and I thought I could drive there and promote my first book on the way in a few cities there and back. The drive was through Detroit and Chicago to Minneapolis, a great opportunity to get exposure in these large markets and those in between.

Everything was going well until the last day of the seminar weekend. I started to feel a lot of pain in the prostate area. The next morning I had to set out for television and radio interviews in Chicago and I had a fever. That night in Chicago I was deathly sick with a high fever but managed to pull off the interviews the next morning. The drive home took two days and was mostly a blur. On arrival home I went to bed and stayed there for several days in a feverish state.

I realized that I had asked for help from my spiritual guide, so I accepted what was transpiring. I seemed to be in an altered state for days feeling like I was in one continuous contemplation. I was able to ask questions and the answers would present themselves, almost like I was in conversation with experts. I discovered that the root of my prostate problem was my attitude around sex. I needed to be more giving. The challenge was that I considered myself to already be a very giving partner. Yet Spirit was saying to me that there is another step, another better way to be a loving partner and that I had to take the next step, moving into greater selfless giving.

This dawned on me in my darkest moment in a fever, but the illness changed my resolve to make the attitudinal changes, now that I understood the subtly of the issue. Soon after making the resolution to change, my fever lifted and I was back in the land of the living!

It taught me how subtle these shifts can be and how the major effects of being out of sync just a little bit can send us into disease.

So the process of fine-tuning our thoughts and the resultant behaviours can have a profound effect on our overall health. This experience buried deep within the overall pattern of lust taught me how vital it is to search out and then heed the message that is hidden in our illness.

Exercise: Making Better Choices

To move forward, making better choices (being more discriminating) in thoughts, words, and deeds ask yourself:

> Am I in balance in giving and receiving love?
>
> Am I honoring myself as Soul?

Impatience and Healing

Impatience is another major theme in healing. Time heals all things, they say. And it is true. Impatience is a mild form of anger, of resistance to the natural flow of life. Impatience is saying, I want this to happen on my schedule, not yours or not Spirit's. Impatience leads to irritation and annoyance and can escalate upwards from there into other forms of anger.

Impatience and its other recognizable forms like "being bothered", "taking umbrage", and "quarrelsomeness" can scatter the concentration of the mind, and in the form of expressed anger creates confusion and trouble.

Slowing down and recognizing the hand of Spirit in all things is a major theme with many people. Letting go and letting God! How can we listen to the whispers of Soul if we are busy rushing to complete our agenda. There is a need to recognize here that there is an overall plan, a spiritual agenda to life, so we need to slow down and accept the pace that Spirit is providing us. This has not been easy for me as a natural planner in my former business career. But over the years I have learned to set a relaxed, more creative pace for myself that allows me to respond to direction from my highest source.

As previously mentioned, walking and driving can be two very useful metaphors for us. Driving the speed limit and slowing our walking pace in the office or outdoors can help us smell the roses on our journey and make our travel time as important as our arrivals and departures.

Exercise: Moving from Impatience into Tolerance and Forgiveness

To move toward greater tolerance and the ability to forgive easily, ask yourself:

> Why is my way the best way?
>
> What can I learn from difficult situations or events, and other people?

Greed and the Mental Body

When greed, excess and over indulgence manifest in the Mental Body, it clouds the mind to the higher values of life. It hardens the consciousness and can result in behaviours such as hypocrisy, perjury and bribery to name a few. Greed is an extreme form of selfishness and can cause illness in those that need to purify and become more giving Souls, sharing of their time, talents, finances and possessions. As we move along this road of personal change and growth, the subtleties of giving will present themselves as opportunities to give greater service to all life.

Soul's end goal of mastership will take you into this part of your lesson plan whether it is a conscious realization or not. So as part of any feeling of disease, ask yourself, where or to whom can you give more of yourself? For example, this is an excellent counterbalance to the disharmony felt in depression. When one gives from the heart with no strings attached, the extreme focus that the depressed person typically has on themselves can lift, and they can shift into a more balanced state.

Exercise: Moving Into a Consciousness of Service

To shift to a greater consciousness of giving, service and contentment, ask yourself:

> Where can I be of greater service or be more helpful to others in my life?
>
> Can I be content with what I have?
>
> Will I be OK without?

A Hidden Side of Greed

Greed can also be present as dissatisfaction or disappointment, and if this state is allowed to manifest too often, it can result in a general unhappiness with life: there is no lasting appreciation or acceptance of what one has. This general state of unhappiness can then devolve into anxiety. Are you content with what you receive in life, or are you always seeking more? More money, recognition, time, fun and attention, are some of the ways this can be present. In this state of constantly living with the feeling of less, one is unable to feel lasting enjoyment. The antidote is gratefulness and appreciation.

> **Exercise: A Consciousness of Contentment**
>
> To move into a greater feeling of contentment of being, ask yourself:
>
> What am I grateful for today?
>
> How can I lift others up with my positive acceptance of the way things are?
>
> In what area of my life can I love myself more?
>
> How can I grant myself forgiveness and tolerance?

The Subtle Effects of Vanity

Vanity rears its head in very subtle ways such as in the form of desiring public honours and publicity. This is the opposite of humility, a state that Soul is seeking on its journey. An exaggerated I-ness of the mind can cloud one from their ability to listen to others and to one's inner guidance as well. Soul may need to "speak" to one in more direct ways through contemplation or other spiritual practices, and if it is not being heard, changes may be required. These changes may be forced upon the physical body as a state of illness, causing one to go deeper inside to solve a challenge. In other words, the pathway to true healing in this situation may only be found in contemplation or by tuning in to other spiritual signs, as the healing methods Spirit suggests may defy the logic of the mind. As one begins to trust their inner guidance more, they move closer to humility and the acceptance of Spirit in their lives.

One such experience came to me as a career conundrum. I was stuck and nothing was working. In contemplation, I received a message that I needed to do a better job and make a greater effort in my contemplations. I was being directed to give my contemplation time a dedicated focus and more time. This book is the result of that process. I was researching a wide range of career opportunities, but what emerged was this writing project.

Another subtle aspect of vanity is shame. It springs from feelings of inadequacy, sometimes perceived as not meeting the expectations of others. It can result in an overemphasis on correctness or decorum. I am reminded of a golfer who was fortunate to be playing with a top ranked PGA Professional one day. However, every time the golfer made a bad shot he would swear. After a couple of holes of enduring this display, the Pro turned to him and said, "You know, you're not that good to be getting this upset." The golfer needed to accept his playing ability for what is was.

Exercise: Toward Humility

To move toward greater humility in interacting with others, ask yourself:

> Can I listen to others without having to add my opinion(s)?
>
> What makes me feel I'm better?

Attachments to the Old Way of Being

Elements of attachment can also play a strong role in our healing process. Being attached to behaviours, being locked into beliefs, having destructive attitudes, may all have to be shattered in the personal purification process leading to wellness.

Flexibility is the virtue that Soul is craving. It needs one to be open, accommodating and a willing participant with life. Accepting change is wrapped up in this process of gaining flexibility. Soul's journey may take it into realms you have never conceived before and a thought pattern may have to be modified or eliminated along the way. Resistance can mean pain. Or the opposite is also true: pain is resistance to change. (Dustin mentioned this awakening for him in chapter seven.) Where is the change required to remove the pain? Headaches are a great example of thought patterns that are no longer serving us. Migraines are a deeper manifestation, meaning that much more is on the change table that needs to be discovered, then altered in our life.

Attachment likes *respectability*, another false value that may need purification at some point. As we shift our perspective to the Soul viewpoint, we realize that we need to feel comfortable in our own skin, in our self-created conditions and lifestyle. After all, we are unique beings on our own personal path of learning. Again flexibility, fluidity, the ability to go with the flow is what we are learning.

Procrastination, not letting go, hanging on to the old conditions can also cause problems that emanate from the Mental Body. Soul is seeking a higher consciousness. That is Its path, and so the ability to get on with things is essential. Hanging on to our comfortable situation can manifest in a form of rigidity in the body such as arthritis, or joint problems etc.

Exercise: Flexibility

For letting go and moving toward more flexibility, ask yourself:

Where can I be more flexible in my life?

What can I let go of? If I let go, how will I benefit?

The Mind-Body can sure have its effects on our physical body and our overall harmony or vibration. As the subtle aches and issues arrive, it is our cue to go searching, to look for where the cause or causes may lie. Life becomes a moving target for those seeking spiritual liberation in this lifetime. Veronica's discoveries about how her thought patterns contributed to her neck pain also led to other beneficial career changes, bringing more joy into her work in the process of letting go.

The Law of Attraction (Law of Attitudes)

Thoughts are very powerful things. What you think, you become. Every thought forms into a future condition. This is why negative thoughts can be very destructive to the body and to your health. These thoughts may be subtle, so much a part of your make-up, you haven't even noticed them.

Negative thoughts are interpreted by your being in the opposite way than you would expect and so understanding the Law of Attraction (sometimes called the Law of Attitudes) is vital to your health and well-being. When you say to yourself, "I don't want to be fat" what your mind carries as a picture is, "I want to be fat." You are left with the residual image of the negative aspects of that statement in your mind to manifest. When you say, "I don't want to get Cancer," the picture you carry is, "I want to get Cancer." Using negative terms of reference can be very damaging to your health! When we create a picture in our minds, these thought vibrations will eventually manifest and the picture comes into visibility in our lives. So, to attract health, you need to be positive about your health. You need to create positive images that can manifest.

Negative thoughts have to go. You need to find a new vocabulary that defines your world in positive terms. You want to be fit, healthy and vibrant, so the negative descriptions need to be abandoned. This means, that what you wish for becomes a positive postulate in your life. State what you want, not what you don't want. This is how the Law of Attraction works. What you say about yourself becomes an image, a picture in your mind, so fill your mind with positive images that can be developed. Know that every thought you have, manifests into a future condition. You are creating your future in your present thoughts.

Actions are also vital. As like attracts like, to get love, you need to give love. To get respect, you need to give respect. To have a harmonious life, you have to be harmony. Positive images and actions manifest as positive results.

Your body always follows the commands given by your mind. Such inner promptings as your thoughts, emotions, feelings, desires, drives, likes, and dislikes serve as the software with which your cells are programmed on a daily basis. Through the mind-body connection, your cells have no choice but to obey the orders they receive via your subconscious or conscious mind. As DNA research has recently proved, you can literally alter your DNA's genetic setting and behavior within a matter of a moment. Your DNA listens to every word you utter to yourself, and it feels every emotion you experience. Moreover, it responds to all of them. You program yourself every second of the day, consciously and unconsciously. If you choose to, you can rewrite the program in any way you want to, provided you are truly self-aware.

Andreas Moritz, author of Cancer is Not a Disease, It's a Survival Mechanism

Exercise: The Law of Attraction

Develop a statement about yourself that reflects three or four key positive qualities you wish to be and start the statement with "I am." Notice that this is in the present tense.

Here are three examples:

    I am happy, healthy, content and creative.

    I am free, wise, successful and loving.

    I am confident, vibrant, and relaxed.

Once you have developed your positive statement, write this statement out fifteen times each day. This will set in motion great changes in your life, building powerful images to manifest in your life. My favourite is: *I am healthy, wise, happy and free.*

Exercise: Positive Thoughts

This exercise is a mental fast. On your chosen day, resolve to think and speak <u>only</u> positive thoughts. Support the ideas of others with positive comments and suggestions – nothing negative. This exercise will shift your vibration and lift you into new realms of being. You will become a positive force in the lives of others as well, just by your example.

Stress, the Silent Killer

In today's fast-paced world, we have become accustomed to stress. It's simply a part of life in Western countries. Some people actually create stress to feel like they are accomplishing a degree of success. As an example I've heard some doctors load up their schedules for this reason. Working long hours in business can also be a badge of honor, and the busier one is, the more the ego is fed.

 Movement into challenging or unknown conditions also brings stress. Originally the word was created by Hans Selye to mean 'change.' Whatever the cause of stress, we now know how destructive it can be on health. Stress can creep into our life and build up very subtly, so inconspicuously in fact that we don't even know it is there, or we simply aren't aware of its presence. But it is creating disharmonies and imbalances in our bodies that can manifest as overt health conditions. Stress from my point-of-view is about 'my will be done.' It is mind over heart, pushing the envelope so to speak. We are driven to succeed, to accomplish, to earn, to not fail, to be better, to accumulate and much more. We need to take a step back and pause. What is life all about? Is it about the things of life, or the qualities of life? Which is it for you? Have you been caught up in the pace of life? Remember, you are different from the crowd. You need to be looking at your life in your own way, through your own lenses, not through the lenses of other's expectations. Perhaps it's time to set your own agenda and pace?

Letting go is key, as well as slowing down. What would happen if you worked more creatively as opposed to trying to produce a volume of work? Slowing down enables one to work from the viewpoint of Soul. This is the source of great ideas, inspiration, and intuitiveness. Which is better; the power of a big idea, a wonderful insight, or high work production? Maybe knowing that you want to transition to being a more creative being will give you the incentive to make changes and reduce your stress. Creativity cannot flourish in a stressful environment. Modern companies have now incorporated gathering places into their work environments for collaboration and to help staff de-stress and laugh a little. Others have included fitness and sports facilities for the same purpose. Some have even built contemplation, meditation and prayer rooms for their people, a strong indication of the awareness that poor staff health, absenteeism and lower productivity can result from stress.

So how can you make changes? Visualization in contemplation can be a big aid to reducing stress, reducing the impact on one's immune and cardiovascular systems. I'm certain that the high incidence of heart attack in our society is in part related to suppressing the heartfelt desires of Soul.

Exercise: Reducing Stress in Your Life.

With everyone you meet in your day, give them more of your time and a smile. Treat them like part of your extended family and enjoy the moments together. Unconditional love is diminishing in our fast-paced world, so bring it back with your new expanded meaning of family to include everyone in your wide circle of relationships as family.

At the same time, make a conscious effort to slow your pace of walking and driving. Count your travel time as important time, not just transit time. Make it a time to muse, contemplate, and decompress. Leave for meetings ahead of schedule so you have plenty of time to chill before your connection. It is much healthier living in a relaxed manner. If you need to, to accomplish this, take something out of your day to make room for your new pace. If you are rushing, you will never have time to give your new "family" at every turn in your day.

Thoughts lead on to purposes; purposes go forth in action; actions form habits; habits decide character; and character fixes our destiny.

Tryon Edwards, American Theologian, author of *The New Dictionary of Thoughts*

Now I invite you to move to Part IV which sheds light on how we can begin the process of discovery and working with several tools at our disposal.

Part IV

Solving Puzzles: Uncovering Root Causes

In creating your own path to well-being you are consciously setting out to discover more about yourself. You are playing a very active role in seeking out what needs to change about yourself and your life.

11

Tapping the Creative Power of Soul

Maybe you are searching among the branches

for what only appears in the roots.

Rumi

Roger's Quest

I first interviewed Roger eight years ago for my book, *Thriving with Spiritual Intelligence*. I chose his story for my chapter on taking responsibility for your life in that book and I included it in the introduction of this book. Roger has been living with Multiple Sclerosis for a number of years, and doing all he is able to do to manage and heal his condition, to work with it, learn from his situation, and grow spiritually. I admire his positive approach to the disease and what he has been able to accomplish as Soul on his human journey in this lifetime.

Writing this book a few years later I felt an urge to check in with Roger, revisit his journey and see what he is dealing with today and where this is taking him. As an example, physically a decade ago, Roger was cycling between cane and walker to assist his mobility. Today, he tells me he relies on his walker, but can use his spirit stick for short distances.

When I asked about his general situation, Roger related to me his latest experience: "I had been experiencing electric shocks in my right temple and jaw on and off for the last six years," he told me. "It would come and go so I thought they were part of my M.S. condition symptoms. About three months ago these shocks became extremely painful. On one day it was so painful I could not open my mouth and for three weeks the pain was so great I could not talk! I did everything in my power to try to solve the problem. Roger has a strong spiritual practice after years of dealing with M.S. which includes regular contemplation. "I was asking the Universe, my spiritual guide, for help. I like to push to get better faster, but I've had to have patience and get through one day at a time," Roger told me.

Searching for Answers

"I searched the web for information, for example, searching on 'MS electrical shocks,' and I was able to verify it could be caused by MS. During this time I was continuously asking and getting messages from others, some in the form of Waking Dreams, (signs and audio messages) about what I needed to do. Doing this talking with others about my condition, I was connected to clove oil. Friends had used it with remarkable results and I began to use it. However, I was in so much pain I ended up in hospital where x-rays were taken. These pictures revealed the condition was bad teeth, not M.S. and two teeth had to be removed. Later, an Internet search also showed that these shocks can also be caused by decayed teeth.

"Then a friend, who was in the habit of forwarding health information to me, sent me an article one day out-of-the-blue about a product I'd never heard of. I was immediately drawn to it. The web site talked about healing the body with consciousness. It was called Oralive (Dental Regenerative Elixir), an all-natural oral balancing paste. The web site says the product contains high vibrational energies which I found extremely interesting. I immediately ordered on line. It's a clay-like substance and I swish it for an hour at a time and it has really helped stop the pain, but I now know I'll need three other teeth removed.

Being Open to Receive

"Even though I'd had these milder electric shocks for six years, all of these events have got me to understand it was my teeth. So by contemplating and asking for direction, all these connections together got me to the point of receiving the Oralive email and being open to it. Over a process of many years and being connected with a spiritual guide and trusting the information, allowed me to once again ask for help and accept it in this situation," he told me.

When I asked Roger to comment more about his guidance, he replied, "What I've been able to understand is that love is endless, and when I reach a new plateau, there is even more love. This comes with more insights."

We talked about the protection people sense when they are in challenging situations. "I don't think of protection anymore," he stated. "If you need to be protected, it's negative because you've created it yourself. If I have love in my heart, I don't need to think of protection. I'm not afraid of anything – I'm not running away from it – I'm not thinking about it to draw it to me," he mused.

Roger is continuing to pay attention to his diet, consuming less sugar these days. "In the past I tried many different diets with little effect – but I think I'll have to go back to it. Generally, I'll use a muscle test to see if something is good or bad for me. If I'm inspired to check out something I'll muscle test it, again asking for guidance all the time, then relying on the guidance.

"It all works to being more connected with spirit – letting go of impatience. The less stress I have emotionally, the better my body is.

Contemplation - A Deeper Search Within

"This whole M.S. experience has helped me search deeper within myself by modifying my beliefs. It's not complete yet, but I'm closer to my Self and to being a lot more spiritual. As an example, the need for anger to get things done has moved to a more relaxed approach today. I have more insights as a result and things are a lot clearer as to how to get things done, like daily chores. For instance, it's a lot easier driving when I'm peaceful, and it allows me to be more open.

"I'm loving myself more – I love my Self, my body, my experience. It helps the day to go a lot easier. I listen a lot to others now to help them overcome difficulties.

"What I've realized through this journey is that I'm not alone. It's better to operate as a team member. I'm always asking for assistance. I'd advise others not to be shy. I'm grateful for people who help me, such as asking me if I need a door opened, or to take me somewhere. Being more connected with others is key. And it's important to be present in the present time when with people. When I couldn't talk for three weeks, I had to rely on sign language and written language. I had to develop more patience because I had to deal with people not understanding me. Then I had to ask myself: 'Is it that important?'

"I've realized that giving thanks for the food I'm going to eat that has been prepared with love, helps to digest it and to appreciate the food more."

It's All About Love

When I asked Roger if he's made new discoveries on the way, he replied: "There are so many. I've learned to let go of what has happened in the last moment, and focus on what I should do now. This means living in the moment and being open to Spirit. That's how you live in the moment – being open."

"There are laws for each different plane; the energy is different on each plane. You have to know which plane you are on (Physical, Emotional/Astral, Causal, Mental) and follow these laws. I find it interesting, the more love I have, the easier it is to operate on a higher level and accept others. People are able to discuss with me what they need to do, and I can just listen, and they come to their own conclusions.

"All in all, I believe I'm here to reach a higher state of love. Out of love comes patience, tolerance, teamwork and there is more joy and more excitement to life. The more love you have, the more love you have in these other areas."

∼

The Power of Going Within

If you truly wish to solve your challenges in life, as Roger's experience shows us, you will want to go within and tap the Creative Power of Soul. There are two methods that appear to be interchangeable in leading you to a greater ability to listen within yourself, to expand your consciousness and enjoy spiritual connectedness: meditation and contemplation. However for the seeker of wisdom there is a difference in the methods. The meditative technique as given by Eastern teachers is practiced by sitting still and gazing into the Third Eye and viewing what may be given to the meditator. It is basically a passive approach in trying to draw God-realization into oneself to attain oneness with God. This method is suited to the slower Eastern world lifestyle and can be a challenge for the Western lifestyle which is faster-paced.

Contemplation is quite different. In this practice, one begins by sitting or lying down. The contemplation can start by closing the eyes and taking a few deep breaths to relax. Chanting a spiritual sound (such as HU or Om) to spiritualize the consciousness can help your contemplation experience although it is not necessary. In contemplation one may gently place their attention on their Third Eye also referred to as the screen of the imagination. During this time of inward reflection, the person can look for inner spiritual light or listen for inner spiritual sounds, or visualize something like a goal. Use of the imagination is key. During contemplation, one can also focus on ideas, challenges, thoughts, or a spiritual principle etc. Some describe contemplation as a form of wondering about something. It is different from Eastern meditation in that it is an active process of inner exploration. The key is bypassing conscious thinking, getting above the mind so to speak, and accessing the soul perspective.

Contemplation is one of the greatest tools of personal discovery I can offer you in tuning in to your inner being, gaining a higher perspective and seeking answers. It is a gentle process of going inward to connect with Soul and Spirit and is a key vehicle to access your creativity and get the answers, direction and guidance you need. You want to go the highest source, Soul. Soul is an integral part of the body of Spirit and so if a question can be asked, there is always an answer available. So the more proficient you are at contemplation, the better your access to intuition, insight and guidance.

The mind is really a tool of the human self and runs on its own learned tracks. So it can only play back its thoughts from a memory bank of its own experiences. Think of the mind as a computer and Soul as the computer operator. In solving life challenges, you will want to get above this pool of mind experiences and tap the creative power of Soul. This is the source of true innovation, insight and fresh ideas. So, creativity is going beyond the limits of the mind, and contemplation is a path you will want to use in your healing process.

Contemplation as a Spiritual Exercise

Just like our muscles need exercise to stay in shape, so do our inborn spiritual abilities. Everyone has these abilities lying dormant within them but very few actually develop and use them. These abilities are a key to developing your personal path to wellness and include the following benefits:

Heightened creativity;

The shift from decision-making to the ability to make conscious choices;

Being calm under pressure;

Knowingness, often of what is best for you and what is not;

Elevated awareness;

A strong sense of Intuition;

Recognizing and trusting outer Signs and messages when they present themselves;

Better problem-solving, the ability to see solutions or the way forward;

Tuning in to what dreams are saying and reflecting back to you;

Seeing the hand of Spirit working in your life;

Gaining a greater trust in the inner nudges and messages you receive, and,

Having a higher perspective on life and its events.

Effective contemplation is an active process and can be called a spiritual exercise. It has a purpose. It is relaxing and effortless, but it does require discipline. It means taking the time to be in a relaxed and receptive state to tune in to the whisperings of Soul. This can often run counter to our busy lives and our worldly training. By this I mean that our natural instincts are toward outer action, not inner exploration. How about you? Are you more comfortable with reading books, googling information and talking to others? This is all good, as long as it does not crowd out the time you need to set aside to contemplate – to tune inward.

Think of yourself as having three minds: the heart (your gateway to Soul's wisdom), the gut and your thinking abilities. Try to use all three faculties in order to maximize your creative potential in your healing process.

How to Contemplate or Do a Spiritual Exercise

This is the key; to set aside time each day for your inner worlds exploration, tapping your creativity. Find a time that is beneficial to you where there is an opportunity for quiet, without distractions. It could be first thing in the morning before work, or it could be at lunch hour if you can close a door to an office or private space. It could be after work upon first arriving home, or it could be just before bedtime. Choose a time that is practical for you. This is your personal time. And it is the time you have set aside to tune in to your personal wisdom. No matter what you are healing from, you will need this time. It will accelerate your healing cycle.

Next, get comfortable either sitting or lying down, as long as you do not fall asleep. Close your eyes and relax. Have an agenda for your contemplation in mind such as a question, or a visualization. Allow your contemplation to carry forward in two parts. First, the active exercise which is forming the question, and second, asking it, or, doing your own guided visualization.

Exercise: Visualizing a Treatment

In contemplation, see yourself at the office of your doctor or healing practitioner. Observe yourself entering the office and then meeting with the practitioner. Visualize a treatment, or imagine a conversation about your challenge. The imagining process is powerful, effortless and carries an endless array of possibilities. The key is to set your contemplation in motion in an active way and run with it.

The second part of your contemplation is less active but still attentive. At this point you begin to participate in the conversation, or you begin to hear answers to your question. Or you may see images, colors, or hear words. Within these contemplative impressions could be the seeds of a direction you may wish to take. Feel free to ask yourself questions about these experiences and more information may present itself.

Give Yourself Contemplation Time

This contemplative process takes time and it may take you several days or weeks to begin to feel that you are getting results. But don't give up. Soul will make itself heard. The key will be for you to trust what you are getting or experiencing, and this comes with practice. You may even want to confirm what impressions you are feeling over a few contemplations just to be sure.

Know that this process is about bypassing the mind. As mentioned before, the mind only knows what it has been programmed to know through its past experiences, so the mind may deny or discredit the information or direction you receive. Therefore the process of verifying insights is completely valid. In the end, you will be combining the directions you set for yourself by working with all "three minds" – your heart, your gut feelings and your logical mind as mentioned above.

Now I'd like to offer you a way to supercharge your contemplations!

The Power of HU

Sound has been used over the ages for upliftment and inner attunement, to experience a connection with Spirit or the Creator. Many churches include choir and pipe organ music to stir this feeling of connection with the Divine. Monks of many religious traditions have used chants for this purpose such as Gregorian chants or Buddhist chants, and many native cultures have used songs and chants for upliftment too. As you have seen in several of the healing stories previously presented, singing HU is one of the ways to experience this spiritual connection. Others have found or been taught other word-sounds for this purpose such as Om or Aum.

HU is an ancient name for God or the Creator. Just saying this sound carries with it the highest vibration possible and imparts it to our being: It acts like a tuning fork, bringing us into greater harmony with Soul and with God. HU is non-denominational, is used in many cultures around the world, and has been experienced for thousands of years. It is a key spiritual tool millions have used before our time, and it is a special spiritual tool available to us today.

When you couple the sound of HU with your contemplation, you have a most powerful combination of tools to access your highest wisdom.

HU is pronounced like the man's name Hugh, or the color reference "hue". It is sung in any note in a long drawn out breath, like HUUUUUUUUUUUUUUU, until your breath is finished. HU can be sung aloud, whispered, sung under your breath, or even silently in your mind. In combining singing HU with contemplation you are combining the upliftment power of this sound with contemplation to access your truth, your highest perspective.

I like singing HU because it is effective and simple and can be sung out loud or silently to yourself to help cleanse and uplift your state of consciousness and to gain broader or deeper insights. However, if you are comfortable with another sound and it lifts you into higher states of awareness, please make a substitution and use your own sound.

Oliver's Gift of HU

Oliver is a personal trainer with a very unique service offering. He is a holistic trainer. "I deal with the physical, emotional, mental and spiritual aspects," he told me. "For me to train, I want to be in optimum shape – I want to be more aware and have a healthy self on all levels. By doing this it gets me where I'm going with a lot less wear and tear," he said. "With me, it's becoming aware in the knowing state so you don't have to experience things in the physical state. So I eat right, I hear and sense what I'm to do on the inner dimensions – intuition, insight and knowingness are the result. This is what I like to pass on to my clients."

When I asked Oliver how this affects his client relationships, he responded, "When I start with a new client, I tell them my overall approach to training is on these four levels; physical, emotional, mental and spiritual, and that I use the HU. I let them know I sing it for many reasons and suggest they may also want to use it to help themselves. I tell them, 'It's non-denominational and connects you to your highest self.'

"When I accept a new client it's a process that unfolds over the next six months. I plant spiritual seeds. That's simply being who I am most of the time. Naturally, some clients are more open to this approach than others, and at the beginning of a new client relationship, I never know how things are going to go with my body-mind-emotions-spirit program method.

"One day I asked myself what I should give my client, George, for Christmas, and the answer I received was to give him the book, *HU The Most Beautiful Prayer.* So I took a risk and gave him a copy. Sometime later, I picked him up in my car to take him to a workout location and I had the HU playing in my car. I usually turn the volume way down when I have clients in the car, but for some reason, I hadn't adjusted the volume. George sat there quietly for a while and then turned to me and said, "I did my HU this morning." I was floored. He had taken up the practice!

Ted Finds the HU

Oliver continued, "On another occasion, I started with a new client couple. Molly was open to my overall approach and was receptive when I talked about singing HU. She was looking for more in life, but her husband, Ted, was not. He was a former professional athlete, a large man, soft-spoken and gentle but closed to the spiritual side of things feeling it was a bunch of Malarkey.

"Then he had an accident while working out which pulled his heel, aggravating an old injury. He ended up in a series of ten physiotherapy sessions. These sessions turned out to be extremely painful, the most pain Ted had ever experienced in all his years of injuries. He told me he would be lying face down as the therapist used a laser gun in the treatment and he screamed so loud he had to smother his face in a pillow."

Ted related this to Oliver about four sessions into the series. When he heard this, Oliver asked inwardly what he could do. His inner answer: Share the HU. "So I did," Oliver told me. "I told him singing HU can heal, uplift and possibly help with the pain. I gave him a little yellow card with 'HU' on it."

The next day Ted was once again on his stomach on the treatment table. He lay there and positioned the HU card so he could look at it, and he began to sing HU and continued singing throughout the treatment.

When they met for the next training appointment, Ted greeted Oliver with a big grin on his face. "Oliver," he said, "I felt no pain!" Ted sang HU for the last six sessions and felt no pain at all. "Ted is now a lot more open, Oliver continued. "He follows all of my advice now. He has cut out all of his meds and his weight has dropped. He is now open to the spiritual side, to things that are of spirit. Before he was closed but now he's asking me questions. It was later that Molly told me I had almost lost Ted in the beginning over the 'spiritual stuff.'"

Oliver surmised, "I feel like I'm instrumental in bringing Souls to this point of discovery – to the Holy Spirit. I want to leave clients with the HU. Our goal is God, Spirit and the HU. This is what I'm about - the realization that we are the HU, that I am that aspect of Spirit, and the more I align myself with it, the more love, wealth, and happiness flows in my life. My abundance is based on my willingness to be the HU, to be this connector to Spirit.

"This is what makes my job so amazing. This physical self is just a coat. It's not who we are. We can be an instrument of love and self-discovery in helping people find out more of their true self. Knowing this brings joy to my life. I love it!

Asking for Help

A primary step in taking charge of the healing process is asking for help. Reflecting back on his challenge with M.S., Roger now seeks inner direction all the time. You must be clear with your questions so the answers you seek will be clear as well. Asking is also best done as part of a process of self-help and self-examination. That is, your best approach is to ask for assistance in solving your challenge, not to ask for your challenge to be solved for you. You need to take responsibility for your condition, after all you created it in some way and it is now present to teach you something about yourself so you can make changes. Right? So understanding that your healing is a process of discovery and learning, your questions should be framed to facilitate this process.

> **Exercise: Asking for Help**
>
> **Some good questions to ask are:**
>
> What do I need to learn?
>
> What do I need to let go of that is no longer serving me?
>
> How can I change and grow to be a better person?
>
> How can I love more?
>
> What do I need to bring into my life to improve it? Could this be a quality of love? (See list in the Appendix.)
>
> Can you please help me solve this challenge in the way you see fit? (Here you are asking to be connected to information, people or other resources that can help you solve your challenge.)
>
> These types of questions imply a partnership with Spirit. You are seeking guidance and taking responsibility for your healing, rather than simply asking for a healing or general help. By taking charge, you are actually accelerating the healing process. Ask yourself, How long do I want to be in this situation? What am I willing to do to move through this condition?

This process of asking penetrating/probing questions will move you out of your traditional comfort zone and into the world of total responsibility. You do everything you can do to solve your challenge.

Who to Ask?

Asking for help from your highest source is a personal choice. You could direct your request to Spirit, or the Holy Spirit, or the Life Force. You may have a religious figure that you call upon for help such as Jesus or Muhammad. You may call upon God or by any name such as Allah, or there may be a spiritual guide or Master in your life that you can call upon for assistance.

Now be prepared to receive!

How to Receive Answers to Your Questions

Spirit (or Its chosen name for you as discussed above) speaks to us in many ways. The key is to be aware of these ways and the messages when they present themselves.

There are an infinite number of paths you can take, and your path will be unique to your need to learn and your overall lesson plan in this lifetime. Therefore, you first of all need to be open to what is presented. After all you are now asking Soul, Spirit or God for guidance, not your mind. You are reaching for answers from on high, otherwise you would have solved your issues by now with brainpower. Not that brainpower isn't useful, but the greater perception here is that you need something new and fresh to face your challenge head on. (Reminder: if you keep on doing what you're doing, you'll keep on getting what you're getting.) Also note that your need to grow spiritually is wrapped up in this healing process and so there may be multiple aspects to your healing; emotional, karmic, mental thoughts, physical impediments and more that are involved.

Unwrapping Your Healing Package

Your healing is a bundle, a package that needs to be unwrapped, so simplistic solutions are always welcomed, but are seldom the case. Consider your disease or condition a mystery package that you need to uncover one layer at a time. And each layer may reveal a new truth to you, creating within you a shift in consciousness, a change in perspective as many of the story-tellers in this book have found. These shifts can also take time to digest into your being, to settle in and become a part of your new you. So be prepared for this journey to take some time. Consider it a voyage of discovery but know that by making a conscious effort to be a partner with Spirit in the process, you can fast-track your learning and healing (often called spiritual healing).

Just like Roger, you become a clue-seeker, a detective on the road to healing, looking for hidden messages in the events of everyday life. Reflect back on the Principle of Creativity in chapter one!

Keeping a Journal

As mentioned in chapter 9, you will want to keep a journal of your healing. This will allow you to record the impressions you receive in contemplations, insights you receive, and of course a record of your treatments, your feelings, and any medicines and other modalities you are involved with. You will also be recording what you feel you are learning on your personal journey. What have you realized? How have you changed lately?

It is best to make a daily entry, even if it is just one line that says how you feel today. Keep it by your bedside to also record your dreams.

I was able to link up a message with a question as follows: I woke up one night with a start. I heard the word, "Shitake" shouted in my ear! I was not looking for any advice at the time but here was this mystery word given to me in such an odd way which I subsequently wrote in my journal. I asked friends if they had heard the word and over the course of a few days I found a friend whose family was originally from China who was able to shed some light on the meaning. She told me that it was a kind of mushroom that had very beneficial enzymes and could help strengthen my immune system. I began to eat these mushrooms for a few months. In looking back into my journal a few months later, my notes illuminated a great deal of stress I had been experiencing due to a marriage break-up, and Spirit was getting me to boost my immune system in advance and during the break-up so that the stress would not lower my body's immune defences. Though emotionally drained, I did not fall into "dis-ease" during this time.

I... recommend to every one of my Readers, the keeping a journal of their Lives for one week, and setting down punctually their whole series of employments (activities) *during that space of time. This kind of self-examination would give them a true state of themselves, and incline them to consider seriously what they are about. One day would rectifie* (rectify) *the omissions of another, and make a man weigh all those indifferent actions, which, though they are easily forgotten, must certainly be accounted for.*

Joseph Addison, English Essayist, Poet and Playwright, 1672-1719

Dreams, the Doorway to Soul

Dreams are a reflection of our waking life and can be a powerful way of receiving information regarding our way forward and what we need to change about ourselves. Paying attention to your dreams can have a profound effect on your healing journey.

When we sleep the body is dormant and at rest. However, the inner aspect of us, our spiritual part called Soul is not. Soul is free to have experiences on the inner planes (also referred to as heavens, spiritual worlds or parallel universes) and indeed does "travel" to different places. It has at its disposal It's other bodies, the astral/emotional body, the causal (karmic) body and the mind body in which to have experiences in these corresponding next higher worlds. It is these memories of our experiences as Soul in the other spiritual worlds that constitute our dream memories. In their purest form these dream experiences are as real and as vivid as our experiences when we are awake. However, these memories of our inner world experiences more often than not, upon awakening, are jumbled thoughts and images.

Our mind has a built-in censoring function that serves to protect the physical body and its present life from information that would be detrimental to Soul's overall growth. This censor will jumble the visual images and substitute other images. And so many of our dreams appear as a muddled collection of images.

The Messages in Our Dreams

These jumbled images and symbols can offer up crucial information so it is important to write them down, even if they appear to be of little value at the time. By asking questions and recording these questions in your journal, it allows you to check back to the questions when recording a dream and then later linking the entries, the question and then the dream. You may be surprised how direct the answers are that are given in your dreams to your questions. So your journal is a key tool for recording your dreams and the symbols that are present in the dreams.

Singing HU (or your spiritual word-sound) aloud or silently just before going to sleep will help to spiritualize your dreams, begin to bring clarity to your dream messages and improve your insight into your dream meanings.

Dreams can be a tremendous source of guidance, often presenting solutions to complex riddles and challenges in very succinct ways.

Signs and Waking Dreams

Spiritual messages, often of help or guidance, can be revealed in the events of ordinary life if we have the eyes and ears to see these vital messages. Life is reflecting back to us all the time, an indication of Spirit working on our behalf. But we need to be aware that these messages are going to be there. An attitude of expectation and anticipation is key. When you ask a question and write it in your journal, be assured that the answer will present itself in some way. Be alert for the sign. It could be presented in your contemplations, in a dream, or in a Waking Dream (a Sign) in the everyday world. The answer could be in a book, on a TV show, in a store, on a billboard etc. So gentle expectation is a rule of thumb here.

A friend of mine was living in another country and had a strong feeling that she should move as she was feeling very unsettled in her present circumstances. So she asked: Where should I go? That day as she was riding along in a bus, she looked up and saw a billboard that said: "Come to Australia." Acting on that message set her on the course of an amazing journey that changed her life. The message felt right and she acted!

In another example of a Waking Dream or Sign, I found myself quite anxious doing a lot of reading about the poor state of the economy. Parallel to this concern, my dog, Oakley, became very skittish about bears in our neighbourhood. If he could smell their scent, he would become very upset and overly protective. The bears like to come into nearby orchards for the fruit in the fall. But this year after five years, Oakley became overly anxious. As I was on a hike one day thinking about the bearish stock market, the connection dawned on me. Oakley was anxious about bears and so was I. I realized that I had to shift away from the negative reading and undue attention I was placing on the bearish stock market. Interestingly, when I let go and moved back into a more balanced state, shedding a hidden anxiety I was feeling, Oakley also let go of his anxiety. We healed each other. I feel he had been picking up on my subtle anxiety and was anxious as well for my safety.

Golden-tongued Wisdom – Audio Signs

Spirit is also working on our behalf by giving us messages and answers through the sounds around us and the voices of others. Sometimes when we are channel surfing on the TV, Internet or radio, a sound clip can offer us insights or answers to our questions. Overhearing words in the conversations of others can also register with us as messages from Spirit. (Remember Caroline's experience when the stranger blurted out, "You have a lot of anger in you.")

A while ago, I was thinking about getting back into real estate and buying a house, after renting during a housing slump, as I walked into a grocery store looking for a large bag of broccoli. The broccoli was eluding me and I ended up asking the grocery manager where I could find it, and he led me over to the shelf. He reached for a bag and checked the expiry date and said, "Hold it for a second." He reached in his pocket and pulled out a sticker and put a 25% discount label on the bag. He was about to hand it to me, then pulled it back, removed the sticker and replaced it with a 50% off sticker! He handed me the bag saying, "It's a little too soon to discount these but what the heck." The expiry date was five days away.

This was such an unusual circumstance I immediately thought there was a message for me in the encounter. It dawned on me that the discounting was a message of more decline to come in the real estate market, and his message, "It's a little too soon," was telling me to place a hold on any immediate real estate purchase plans.

Spiritual Fasting

Fasting has a way of clearing the clutter out of your life like nothing else. It can bring clarity to issues and offer up answers to questions. It can illuminate your dreams, make them easier to remember and draw your attention to Signs that you might have otherwise missed.

I've found that I am "lighter" when fasting, more centered, and more connected. Perceptions are heightened and insights forthcoming. Contemplations can be much deeper and provide clearer answers to the mysteries we seek to uncover.

Detachment is a big key. When we detach from food, somehow we are able to detach on other levels too, and when we let go of our attachments to ideas, emotions, past events that may be hiding guilt, remorse or other feelings, we are just that much freer. Letting go is a very real event, occurring on many levels.

When you are asking questions, asking for insights or guidance, fasting can be a wonderful tool to employ to magnify the effects. I have fasted three different ways, each with varying degrees of effect. Consistency though is of great benefit such as once a week which has been my pattern for many years. And Friday has been my special day.

Three Ways to Fast

The first fast that I practiced was a water only fast for 24 hours. This was very difficult at first but I persevered for several years. I don't practice this fast any more but the pattern is so ingrained in me that I still wake up earlier Saturday mornings hungry for breakfast. (If you are attracted to this type of fast, I suggest you seek guidance from your medical advisor.)

The second fast that I have practiced is the partial fast. This can be done in many different ways. I skipped breakfast and lunch and ate dinner at five o'clock. You can be creative with this by eating only fruit for your meals, or skipping meat for example. It should be enough to create a feeling of detachment from your usual pattern.

The third fast is a mental fast. For me this means keeping my thoughts on my spiritual guide. For you, it could be to keep your thoughts on God, your spiritual leader or some other inspirational spiritual figure. You could also keep your thoughts on the qualities of Divine Love. As well, you could do and say everything with love as you go about your day. This would also translate to your thoughts that would also be loving, never negative. As you can see, this can be a very difficult fast if done diligently. You will be treating people quite differently as you go about your day. You will look more content and will exhibit an uncommon cheerfulness. If doing this fast, observe how people begin to relate to you differently.

Spiritual fasting can be a very powerful aid to your healing process, giving you a different viewpoint, helping you see life from a changed state of consciousness having pulled your mind out of its usual patterns. In the process you can be working off karma by loosening the attachments of your material world.

Letting Go of What Ails Us

In the process of fasting or letting go of certain foods incompatible with our particular constitution, there is a similar process going on in our higher spiritual bodies. When we are in the process of detaching from certain foods or food groups we are also opening ourselves to insights about ourselves and detaching from other habits that are no longer serving us? When I think of the results I've experienced fasting from all foods, certain foods, or even other partial fasts, I've found the action shakes loose other parts that need purification – emotions, thought patterns, and even issues emanating from my past (karma) – and these impurities can get "burned off" as the fasting lightens us and shines a spotlight on the smudges in our character and behaviors.

I know how hard it is to let go of certain foods we enjoy and are a comfort, but in the act of detaching from them I believe it strengthens us in letting go of other aspects of our being that are holding us back spiritually.

Muscle Testing/Applied Kinesiology

Getting the clues we need to move us forward can come from many sources as highlighted above as well as through personal insights, aha moments, intuition and outright advice from medical professionals, family and friends. But we also have the ability to test these sources and their implications. Muscle Testing (Applied Kinesiology) is a good way as Roger has found, to get a degree of validation, to determine if a direction is in harmony with his highest good. You can hold a medicine or supplement in your hands while a friend pushes down on your extended arm. If it gives way easily and indicates little strength, then try it again with another choice. If you discover your arm holds firm when pressure is applied, this could be beneficial for you and your healing. I have done the same thing by writing alternatives on small cards and holding the cards so that I can't see what is written. The same process is followed. The answers may surprise you! There are many sources including Wikipedia.com for how to do Muscle Testing so I have not gone into detail here on how to effectively do it.

Tapping the Creative Power of Soul with Yoga

We all know yoga is good for fitness but it can also be a spiritual practice and a wonderful healing companion. It opens up the body and keeps it receptive and flexible and can be an aid to detoxification. These benefits also translate to other levels of your being – your emotional, causal, and mental bodies. When something changes, opens or expands on one level, it has the effect of initiating a similar action in another part of us - as above, so below. Yoga can be excellent for balancing the energy centers (chakras), and certain postures can have specific benefits for healing and integration on all levels. Most types or brands of yoga encourage inner reflection in postures such as shavasana where one is lying down, or mountain pose which is a standing posture. The breath work in some yoga styles also has the effect of helping one connect to the calm quiet place within.

Spiritual Surrender

A major key to healing is surrender. Life moves in cycles and so when we are in a "down" cycle with an illness, injury or disease we want to be able to connect with whatever we need to bring us back into balance. This is when it is a good time to keep ourselves open to Spirit so that we will recognize the assistance when it is presented through all of the ways presented in this chapter.

Surrender to Spirit is a form of letting go or detachment (let go and let God). In order to surrender, you can say to yourself, *I turn this situation over to Spirit so that I am being more open to what it is that I need to understand about myself, what I need to change, and what divine principle I need to better understand so I can move forward in life.* By this act of surrender you are asking Spirit to lead you into a greater way of life.

When I asked Caroline who surrendered during her healing process from sciatic pain (chapter 8), what surrender meant to her, she replied: "I think of myself driving a bus with all my family and friends on it. I am in control and think that I know what is best for everybody. When I surrender I give up total control of the bus, move back with the others and allow God to drive, knowing that I will receive the highest and best experience for me and so will everyone else. It may not always look like I am going in the right direction or appear to be what I want, but I trust the driver-God.

In surrendering, you need to give over your fears, cares and worries to Spirit. In this process you are becoming a greater vehicle for Spirit, for love. Fears and worries only close the channel, the connection you have with Spirit. You want this partnership with Spirit open so you can respond to what Spirit brings your way. You want to be connected to love and what accompanies this love – spiritual insight and spiritual help.

In this state of spiritual surrender you are relaxed, balanced and working in a higher, more aware consciousness.

Exercise: Surrendering Completely to the Will of God

Go into a contemplation with the purpose of surrendering your situation to Spirit or God. When you are ready in the contemplation, when you feel very relaxed and connected, say to yourself:

I turn this situation with love over to Spirit.

After a few moments, say: *I wish to be more open to what it is that I need to understand about myself.*

After a few more moments ask: *What is it that I need to change?*

Finally, ask: *What Divine Principle do I need to better understand so I can move forward in life?*

Continue to contemplate on letting go of your situation. You can visualize wrapping your situation in a gift box and then handing it to Spirit, your spiritual guide or to God.

Now expect peace and serenity and be open to possible answers flowing into your space in the form of dreams, Signs, being connected to information and more.

Make a daily entry in your healing or spiritual journal.

> **The ultimate value of life depends upon awareness and the power of contemplation rather than upon mere survival.**
>
> Aristotle

The next chapter will give you some ideas on how to look for clues to regain balance and harmony in your complete being.

12

Healing Metaphors: Solving Riddles of Illness, Injury & Disease

In every crisis there is a message. Crises are nature's way of forcing change — breaking down old structures, shaking loose negative habits so that something new and better can take their place.

Susan Taylor, American editor, writer and journalist

Rebecca's Spiritual Signal

Rebecca's world was rocked one day when she returned home from work to find her husband dead. He had died shortly after she had left for work and had been laying there on the floor all day. They had only been married three years. Her life, however, was about to take another awful turn. At the funeral she was asked by friends, "Who is that lady bawling over there?" A little later, the woman approached Rebecca and was very angry with her and it was in that moment Rebecca realized this woman had a romantic connection with her husband! Soon it became apparent her husband had been having an affair throughout their marriage.

Rebecca's life hit bottom. First a tragic loss, then a betrayal. Rebecca later determined her husband could not face leaving her and had a heart attack.

As time went on, Rebecca found that she was the only one who didn't know about the affair. The whole family knew! "I could not tell him what a S.O.B. he was now that he was dead. I could not face this situation. I was really hurt because I trusted him," she told me. "But I knew deep down I had caused this. I used to go out with married men in my younger days," she confessed. "I liked married men because they were safe. One even arrived on my doorstep with his suitcase after leaving his wife. I had to send him home. Now it was payback time."

A Sore Throat – Holding it In

It still didn't make Rebecca's life any easier knowing she had to take responsibility for her betrayal. As time went on, her throat became sore. "It was very hoarse," she recounted. "I finally made an appointment with my doctor six months later. On examination he could find nothing wrong. He had me sit down and asked me, 'What's been happening these last six months?' I broke down in a flood of tears and cried and cried. I told him the whole story. I had been holding back, not expressing myself – all of my sadness, disappointment and hurt. I had no one I could share this with. I couldn't talk about it at work, I had no family at the time and my one close friend was away. I was alone.

"I felt the crying was the start of a healing, getting it out of my system. The doctor didn't give me anything for my throat but he did prescribe an antidepressant. I took a quarter pill a day for two weeks. My throat began to heal and within two weeks it was better. Soon after that I found my current spiritual path which confirmed my thoughts about karma and reincarnation.

Help from Contemplation and Dreams

"Dreams also played a part in my spiritual growth during my healing time following the death and betrayal. One night I had a dream of a beautiful large white wolf. He was standing up on a bluff. I thought he was going to attack me, but instead he attacked the dark side of me, protecting me. It was a spiritual awakening for me." It was at this point Rebecca revealed she was a recovering alcoholic. She had gained sobriety about a year before her husband's death after a friend had introduced her to Alcoholics Anonymous. "The dream was telling me to be careful. It helped me to see how easily I could slip back. It wouldn't take much. I tend to write my dreams in cycles. If I don't journal, a dream will come up that I need to write down, and this pulls me back into journaling.

"After finding my new spiritual path, I felt love. I was on a spiritual high. I had a sense of belonging now. It's the family I never had. This helped me to move past my experiences, the betrayal and anger, and I was able to move forward and let go. I knew it was karma but the contemplations/spiritual exercises I started to practice were the key to moving on. Today, Spirit is such a part of my life and I see it at work in my life all the time now.

"Contemplation is now a tool I use all the time. As a child I would talk to my guardian angel, so contemplation was a natural progression for me. I ask God for help when I need it, but I know I have to help myself first, to have the willingness to do better, to be better. So asking is also a part of my being today. The way it works best for me is gratefulness – to be connected to the higher power."

Shaped by the Past

Rebecca also told me about her upbringing which has had a great influence on her life. Her mother was a poor immigrant that could not afford children. Her mother told her she would try to abort her pregnancies, but Rebecca was born in spite of this. Rebecca would reply to her mother, "I was meant to be."

"I've had to keep a lot inside in my life like watching my mother get beaten and even being beaten myself as a child. I could tell no one. This builds up. The walls build up. I was afraid to express myself."

At age twenty-six, Rebecca was bulimic and in a marriage she had to leave. She began drinking to numb the pain, yet she associated alcohol with fun. It was an escape for her. She carried her drinking into the second marriage, and as she began to feel something was wrong, her drinking increased.

Rebecca continued, "My friend talked me into going to AA when I was ready to face the disease and life around me. When my world fell apart, I resisted alcohol in spite of everything that happened. AA is a spiritual program and connected me with the higher power. It was a stepping stone to my spiritual path today. AA helped me let go of the emotions. I have so much trust in Spirit now. Life has become so much easier, with my daily contemplations which give me my spiritual strength. But I have to continually work at it – to deal with the betrayal, and the alcohol.

"I don't want to go back to where I was. I can't slack off. I want to live every day with gratefulness. I am so happy to be healthy, alive and sober, to be connected to a higher power.

Discovering My Life Mission

"I realize now why I'm here. I have a mission. The little I do helps others. By sharing our experiences, this also helps others. I've discovered I need to let go of the past and live in the present moment. In my experience burning off karma, I got a taste of my own medicine. I felt safe with married men. I never meant to hurt anyone but I still had to pay for this - it was selfish. I was just thinking of myself. With my husband's death and betrayal it all came to a head. It was interesting that day: his sons were working around his house all day and never knew he was dead inside. I was the one who was meant to find him. I needed to have the full effect of that experience.

The Throat Metaphor

"Today my throat acts up from time to time but I've discovered that if I don't get my feelings off my chest, it returns, particularly if I'm tired, stressed or sad. For example, if I start housework and my voice starts changing, I know it's time to quit. If I talk my feelings out, my throat returns to normal. My present husband today is a "controller" and so is my teacher in this respect. My throat comes on unexpectedly and leaves as quickly when I express my feelings.

"My daily contemplations have been a big help in me working with my throat 'messages.' If I sit quietly and sing HU, I'll have an inner connection. It relaxes me and makes a difference in the hoarseness. It calms my voice and my being. My throat is like a barometer telling me to speak up, slow down, and smarten up. All the time I'm getting this guidance."

Seeking and Changing

In creating your own spiritual path to well-being, you are consciously setting out to discover more about yourself. You are playing a very active role in seeking out what needs to change about yourself and your life. You now understand that this life is a purification process and a road of discovery about what is causing disharmony in your body. Often your body is telling you what needs to change in order for you to grow and heal in the process.

A Movie Metaphor

I was intrigued by the story line of the movie, 50/50. Inspired by a true-life experience, it is a comedy centered on a 27-year-old guy who learns he has Cancer, and his subsequent struggle to beat the disease. As with all good movies there is a character transformation in the plot. The main character is portrayed as a very likable character, but with a milk-toast personality. He lets the people in his life walk all over him with their opinions and behaviors.

One day he is told by his doctor that he has a very rare form of Cancer in his spine. When he goes through treatment it is not having the desired results. But as he faces his likely demise he begins to stand up for himself. He has nothing to lose. He faces his mother, his therapist, his friend and his boss, and begins to assert himself, to express himself truly. In effect he is growing a spine. He is developing a backbone!

His surgery is more complicated than expected but as he takes greater control of his life and expresses his true feelings, his recovery also accelerates.

I appreciated the movie as the true story of a disease that had manifested in this young man's back to teach him to "grow a backbone," to stand up for himself - his beliefs and feelings.

My Lower Back Reveals a Subtle issue

Over the course of one summer my lower back area developed a stiffness and was really affecting my golf game. I would do daily yoga stretches but every morning it would take about an hour for my back to warm up and let go of the discomfort. I knew at the time that a stiff, sore or painful lower back was an indication of financial worries or anxieties yet no cause seemed apparent. In a contemplation one day I was wondering if being an avid reader of financial information on the Internet could be the cause of my condition. I didn't feel that I was worrying, but I will admit that I was very involved in how the financial markets were performing and how my investments would fare. But I didn't think my feelings could possibly be causing such a reaction in my body.

So I decided to do an experiment - an information fast. This was hard for me to let go of this "vital" information each day, but I could do it if needed. After all, I rationalized, if I was on vacation I wouldn't be checking prices every day – I'd be out-of-touch from my broker anyway. So I let it all go. And wouldn't you know it, after a few days I woke up and got out of bed without any discomfort! I realized I was more concerned than I thought. The financial information was an overload, obviously affecting me at a vibrational level and the way my body could convince me was through the stiffness in my back.

After being away from my daily dose of information negativity, I realized I was able to stand back from the situation and could see that this constant information diet had little value for me anyways and was also affecting my overall outlook on life. I knew that my financial strategy was already set and no amount of constant checking on the market performance was going to change my allocations anyways. So I learned that even subtle influences like reading certain material or having an inappropriate focus on a subject can be harmful to our overall well-being. Although I had substantially scaled back my financial news, there was more to come, which I'll get to later.

How the Body Talks

On my journey I have found a number of messages that my body conveys through its various parts and these messages can be found in the language and expressions we use, often as figures of speech. Possibly the following suggestions can assist you with your discovery of root causes of imbalances. These ideas merely suggest contemplation seeds, a starting point for you to get a fresh insight into your personal metaphor(s).

Accidents: I find myself with cuts, bruises, or having accidents when I have broken a spiritual commitment or resolution I have made to myself, or I'm ignoring a direction that Soul wants to take, what my heart is telling me.

Bladder: Being "pissed off". Is there a situation in your life that is really bugging you? Is there a person in your life that would fall into this category?

Back (lower): A stiff or sore lower back is a problem that arises for me when I place too much emphasis on financial issues, worrying more and not trusting enough in myself or in spirit.

Ear: What are you not hearing or paying attention to? Are you listening to your heart? Are you ignoring the voice inside you?

Eye: The ego, the I-ness. Is there a possibility that your ego is getting in the way of accepting a change, or accepting someone or their ideas? What do you see in your life? What are you not seeing?

Foot: Feet and legs carry us forward. My foot becomes sore when I am heading in the wrong direction in regard to an aspect in my life. Could you have taken a wrong turn that is not in harmony with your true destiny, the destiny of Soul?

Gut (Bowels): Gut feelings — Are you ignoring these? Are you hanging on to the old? What do you need to let go of?

Hands: Hands hold things. What are you holding on to? Do you need to let go? What are you not holding on to?

Head: What's on your mind? The mind wants control over the heart and gut feelings. Are you listening to your mind and ignoring your gut feelings and heartfelt desires? What is it you *think* you should do that perhaps is not in balance with your heart?

Heart: The center of love. Are you loving yourself enough? Are you giving yourself what your heart desires? Is there a fear holding you back? Is there something you would love to do that you are stifling? What can you put your heart into? Are you giving love to those close to you? Do you love your life? What feels natural?

Hip: Hips hold up our bodies. They are a foundation. Is your foundation being rocked? Do you feel that you are losing your foundation?

Joints: Joints represent flexibility. How resistant to change are you? Flexibility relates to ideas, beliefs, thought patterns, habits, routine and more. Where can you be more flexible in your life? Is there a situation or person that you could be more flexible with? Are you open to change? Is it all good?

Knee: The knee represents the connection between the higher and the lower leg. The metaphor for me is my connection between my higher and lower self. Are you using your intuition? Are you going within for your answers? Are you letting spirit into your life? Are you giving Soul a voice?

Legs: Your legs move you forward. Are you moving forward or are you at rest in your life, work, relationships, home life etc? Leg problems can indicate a need to get on with changes, to step out.

Lips: Chapped lips, sores etc. cause me to ask myself what food or drink has passed between my lips that could be causing problems? Is there a food or drink that is no longer in harmony with your being.

Muscles: Are you moving with ease in life? Are you venturing forth into the new? Could you be holding back?

Lungs: Lungs represent the breath of life, the zest for life. Are you suffocating in your present situation – work, relationships, home life etc? Do you want to spread your wings and fly? What is holding you back?

Shoulder: Shoulders carry loads. "Shoulder that load." "Put your shoulder to the wheel." Shoulder problems can indicate a need to stop pushing on something, an agenda or project that needs breathing room. Are you shouldering too much?

Stomach: What can't you stomach? Are you resisting a change? Is there something you are having trouble digesting (accepting)?

Skin irritations: What are you itching to do? Is there something holding you back? Is someone or something getting under your skin?

Thumb: Our thumbs help us to grip. What do you need to get a grip on? What are you gripping on to too tightly? Are you hanging on to something, a situation or person that you need to let go of? Does your mind have a grip on something that is keeping what Soul wants from happening?

Throat/Voice: This represents our voice, our passions. Are you expressing yourself? Are you able to say what you feel? Are you suppressing the need to express your feelings? Are you telling it the way it is, expressing your truth? Is there a hidden fear holding you back?

A Dream Metaphor

A few months after I'd scaled back my financial reading, I had a disturbing dream that really made me contemplate on what was going on in my life. When I awakened with the dream in my awareness, I silently sang HU to myself to gain a higher perspective and better understand its meaning. In this short dream, I could see that my eye tooth was turning brown. This really shocked me. As I lay in bed that morning, what came to me was that the digestion system relates to what we take in from the external world. The teeth chew what we take in. So I asked myself, What could it be that I am taking in and chewing on that is rotting my eye tooth? Ah, the eye tooth. As I lay there contemplating on that piece of the dream message, I realized it had to do with reading! Of all the reading I do, at that time I was still reading a little financial information and analyses from time-to-time on the poor state of the economy and this "information" presented itself as the culprit. I had cut way back on my financial reading but obviously not enough. I determined the dream was telling me that the subtle effects of this Internet reading would cause me problems, conceivably even causing my eye tooth to rot! In that moment of awakening I decided to fast completely from this kind of information as it obviously was not serving me well, even though I really enjoyed the subject matter – sort of like candy. So it took this dream to get me to fully let go of a subtle yet toxic influence on my being.

Exercise: Finding Your Own Messages

Experiment with practicing some free association with the key words that define the area of your challenge by writing them down on a sheet of paper. Three examples are as follows:

Leg problem: Get a leg up. A leg of a race. My legs carry me places.

Neck problems: Bottle neck. Neck tie party. Necking.

Hair: Bad hair day. Hairy beast, Hair today, gone tomorrow.

> By free associating, playing with words in your vocabulary, you may stumble across an idea worth exploring in contemplation. Soul can be quite clever in sending you a message via the body that you can uncover!

I had a red flare develop above my lip a few years ago. Red to me is a danger colour, a warning sign. It came to me that the danger was associated with what was going in my month due to the location of the flare. In thinking back to what I'd eaten that day, I was able to find the culprit – soup. Although I had said no MSG and the restaurant confirmed they don't use the substance, I found out the soup powder stock base they use contains it. So no more soup in restaurants for me!

My body gave me a warning before a more dramatic manifestation occurred.

Our bodies communicate to us clearly and specifically if we are willing to listen to them. Shakti Gwain, New Age Author

Now I'd like to offer you an array of healing support options, some of which you may be attracted to in helping you get to the root of your disharmony.

13

Finding Your Personal Path

He that will not apply new remedies must expect new evils; for time is the greatest innovator.

Sir Francis Bacon, pioneer of the Scientific Method, 1561-1626

Unlocking the Puzzle Box

Amanda's healing odyssey started the day she noticed a little pimple on the side of her nose. When the eruption appeared she immediately knew it was skin Cancer. She told me, "I had one on my neck before and when it had not healed about a year later, I realized it must be Cancer. A biopsy proved it was. When this one appeared on my nose, I knew," she said. Amanda has been a natural health advocate for over forty years with extensive knowledge of many alternative health regimes. Amanda asked herself, "What am I going to do. It's on my nose!"

She had used black salve before on her neck (also known as Cansema) and got it resolved. But this time she recounted, "I was afraid to use it on my nose. Fears of disfigurement were a preoccupation. I was dithering for quite some time, using essential oils and The Beck Protocol which involved magnetic pulse treatments. These were keeping the skin Cancer under control," she continued.

A Significant Loss Adds More Stress

Then, Amanda's husband Reggie fell ill and was hospitalized on an emergency basis. The stress and trauma of her husband's illness and being a caregiver when Reggie came home took its toll. "I could see how the Cancer had spread over my nose under the skin. I was so focused on Reggie, though, that I just continued with the essential oil and The Beck Protocol treatments." Reggie passed away soon after, adding to Amanda's physical and emotional challenges.

Amanda continued: "After Reggie's Memorial Service, I decided it was time to do something more. I applied a small amount of Black Salve and it ate a big crater on the side of my nose and even ate into the bridge in one area. To help heal the hole, I started taking hyperbaric oxygen treatments on my own. As a natural health advocate, I knew I had to walk the talk so I wanted to clear the Cancer using natural treatments. I'd also seen a naturopathic doctor and a medical doctor. The medical doctor had referred me to a surgeon. Upon examination, the surgeon wanted to immediately book a surgery date as the Cancer in the tip of my nose was quite large. My naturopathic doctor referred me to a naturopathic specialist in Cancer with European training in a major city five hours away. I booked a telephone appointment with him and he gave me a regime to follow. I chose to go this route so I called and postponed the surgery. I wanted to give the natural way a chance to work. The regime involved daily juicing, a healthy diet without sugar or processed foods, supplements, intravenous Vitamin C, Mistletoe injections, and I continued to use The Beck Protocol.

"I got a new surgery date two months in the future. Six weeks later, there was no progress with my natural approach so I scheduled an appointment to see the naturopathic (Cancer) doctor in person. I had a big fear of losing my nose at this point and the worry often made it difficult to get to sleep. I would sing HU to calm myself and eventually drift to sleep. The night before my appointment, I sang

HU. I sing HU all the time to connect with my inner being and spiritual guidance, but this evening I especially needed to fully surrender. That night I really embraced the fear. I asked my inner guide for help, for guidance. I acknowledged my fear and then truly surrendered the outcome.

A Vital Dream

"That night after falling asleep I had a significant dream. In the first part of the dream I was driving from a large island to the mainland with a friend who I perceived as my inner guide. Upon reaching the mainland I needed to park the car. I planned to park at a shopping mall. When I got out of the car, however, I was in a quiet wooded area beyond the shopping mall. Someone called my name – it was a woman I knew. I looked at her and in the background there was a building with three service bays with a man standing at each bay. I started walking with my friend. We headed up a steep sandy bank to get to a road above us. I kept slipping back near the top. My friend encouraged me to continue as another friend was waiting with a car at the top. That was the end of my dream.

"When I saw the naturopathic doctor the next day, he could see the Cancer cells easily as I had been using Curaderm, another salve for skin Cancer that had peeled the surface skin off my nose. I kept my nose covered as it looked so red and raw. He suggested I go ahead with surgery saying that a lot of natural therapies don't work as well with Basal-cell carcinoma (Cancer) as it is slow growing. He mentioned the Cancer in the tip of my nose was particularly large and he could see the areas further up my nose as well. (Like the Black Salve, Curaderm destroys Cancer cells without affecting healthy cells.) My dream began to make sense to me. In the dream, natural therapies were the island and Western medicine was the mainland. I was heading in that direction. So I returned home thinking I would go ahead with the surgery. The next day, I reflected further on my dream. I associated the friend I walked with as well as the one waiting up on the road with healthy eating and natural health. But I was not getting up the steep bank to the road as I kept slipping near the top. I realized the dream was telling me the program I was on would not be enough to get me to my goal of clearing the Cancer. Then I reflected on where I was parked—a quiet area, not at the mall which represented a mainstream solution. That realization about what the dream was telling me, made me take another look at the service bays and the three men standing out front. I knew these men were spiritual masters helping to guide me. The service bays told me there was something I still needed to discover. I was now on alert for Spirit to show me the next step.

"Three days later I was at the Naturopathic doctor's office getting intravenous Vitamin C therapy. During treatment, I struck up a conversation with a fellow who was there with his elderly mother. It turned out he was working with a group of doctors to make their pharmaceutical product for Cancer better known. He told me the product had a lot of research behind it. I was immediately interested. He invited me to give him a call and he wrote his number down on a slip of paper for me. Later I called and left a message, but after several days, he still had not returned my call. I was anxious to hear from him. It was at this point I had another dream. In this dream, I'm visiting with him, his mother and sisters. They had all been at the naturopath's office that day. There was a warm feeling among us. This dream assured me that this product was the one I needed.

Finding the Missing Puzzle Piece

"A few days later I got a call back from him – he had been away on a trip. His new product was Careseng, a concentrated Ginseng product. It is taken intravenously as well as orally via gel capsules. He put me in touch with a medical doctor who arranged for my Naturopath to substitute the new product for the Intravenous Vitamin C I was being treated with.

"At this point I could see the relevance of the service bays in my first dream. I realized they are like the stations you go in to when getting intravenous treatment. In other words, the chairs in a row are like a series of service bays. This product was not mainstream (the mall); it was represented by the quiet area where I found myself parked. It was suggested I'd need four months for the Careseng treatments, and so I once again delayed the surgery to give the Careseng a chance.

"Four months later I went to see the surgeon to see what Cancer remained in my nose. All along he was very open to what I'd been doing with my alternative approaches and he was willing to book surgery for the third time. His office received a cancellation for surgery ten days hence so I was slotted for that time which allowed me to move forward quickly with surgery—a little miracle. Surgery resulted in a skin graft from my shoulder onto my nose. When the surgeon met me to go over the biopsy report he had a huge grin on his face. He told me there had been considerable scar tissue in the one area but there was no sign of Cancer in my nose!"

Amanda's Keys to Healing

When I asked Amanda about some of the keys to her healing she replied: "I couldn't have done this without the HU. Singing HU helped me let go of the fear when it came up. I felt at the time I needed to shoulder it, but that night when I surrendered more than I ever had, I had a beautiful feeling when I let go of the outcome – the fear of disfigurement. The strength I gained from doing daily contemplations (spiritual exercises) helped me reach that attitude of surrender.

"My pivotal dream also helped me to be able to deal with the fears easier as they came up after that time. The love I experienced at times during my journey helped, including the love and emotional support from my family, and the dreams also allowed me to tap into this love that surrounds me and that I'm capable of giving back. Because of this love, I've learned to love.

"My journaling every evening has also been a big help. For me it's magic. When something is niggling at me, when I write it down and look at it honestly, it helps me surrender easily. When I do this, I'm really writing to my inner guide. A few minutes later after getting it down I feel healed."

Amanda spoke about her overall experience and about other realizations she uncovered. "In this healing process I had to deal with the loss of my husband. I can see more and more I have definitely allowed myself to feel the grief. My mom died just before my twelfth birthday. Coming from a stoic background, very soon nobody talked about her in the presence of me or my younger sisters. That was their way of protecting us. I discovered many years later that I had buried grief. With Reggie passing I was using childhood mechanisms to keep from feeling the grief. My nose issue allowed the emotional part of the grief healing process to take place concurrently. I was looking for help to identify emotional issues that were a part of this: anger played a subtle role too, and feeling abandoned."

Amanda talked about some of her major realizations about health, healing and modalities. "I have been so steeped in natural remedies for four decades; I had a bias toward it versus traditional medicine. I had to let go of all of it. I had a fear of medical doctors not supporting me because of my naturopathic beliefs and I had to let go of all of this too. Today I am more compassionate about others going through health challenges and more accepting of their decisions. It took a great deal of discipline for me to go my route and I can now see others may not have the same discipline and so will go the traditional medical route.

The Power of Asking for Help

"Asking played a key role in my journey. It doesn't mean, God, take it away. It means, Thy will be done, and show me the way. I've discovered I have a renewed recognition to experience what I need to experience - to live my life gracefully, to grow in self-mastery, so I can be a better vehicle for Spirit here. Each person has to decide in their own heart what it is they want to do, then go for it. There is no one way. No one method or product was it for me. It was the combination. My initial program took me up the slope almost to the top of the road (in my dream), but the Careseng got me the rest of the way. Everything helped me. All I did was allow the body to heal itself physically, emotionally and mentally – discovering all the things that were needed to allow my body to heal at all levels."

Amanda finished by saying, "I would like to add how grateful I am for the guidance I received when I asked my inner guide for help. Spiritual experiences like the dream that guided me are precious."

Amanda's healing odyssey shows us how to solve a healing puzzle by asking for help, listening for inner wisdom, and being open and flexible to new approaches.

Methods, Modalities and Remedies

As I stated at the beginning of this book, this book is designed as a guide to help you work with many tools that are available today to help you get well and stay well from a spiritual perspective. It is not about providing specific medical advice or about promoting specific modalities. Like Amanda, you need to find your own path to wellness because your present state is a reflection of your unique make-up that has been formed over many lifetimes. And so your health and healing must also reflect the unique nature of your personal journey.

We are fortunate today to have at our disposal a vast spectrum of modalities, healing practitioners, and medicines, in fact an immense range of possibilities that can assist us on our personal road to healing. One must be open, flexible and courageous to follow one's own path. But in the end, your path will lead to harmony and balance because you have created it.

The following is a list of possibilities in addition to pharmaceutical medicines and traditional Western Doctors or Specialists. It is important that one is open to all of the possibilities. Healing is a very personal process and so your path may take you into realms unknown.

I have added an asterisk to those approaches that I feel could assist with diagnosis, helping you uncover the underlying causes of your challenge(s).

*Acupressure: The use of finger pressure on specific points along the body to treat ailments such as tension and stress, aches and pains, menstrual cramps, arthritis.

*Acupuncture: Fine needles which are inserted at specific points to stimulate, disperse, and regulate the flow of vital energy, and restore a healthy energy balance. In addition to pain relief, acupuncture is also used to improve well being and treat acute, chronic, and degenerative conditions in children and adults.

Alchemical Healing: The fusion of diverse and innovative techniques of shamanism with energetic healing and the principles of alchemy to create a method applicable in today's world for physical healing, therapeutic counselling, and spiritual growth.

Alexander Technique: A method that works to change movement habits in our everyday activities, it is said to be a simple and practical method for improving ease and freedom of movement, balance, support and coordination. The technique teaches the use of the appropriate amount of effort for a particular activity, giving you more energy for all your activities.

Anthroposophical Medicine: It is a method which, before attempting to investigate the spiritual worlds, first develops psychic powers not normally used in daily life or in current scientific research.

Aromatherapy: With the use of "essential oils" distilled from plants, aromatherapy treats emotional disorders such as stress and anxiety as well as a wide range of other ailments. Oils are massaged into the skin in diluted form, inhaled, or placed in baths. Aromatherapy is often used in conjunction with massage therapy, acupuncture, reflexology, herbology, chiropractic, and other holistic treatments.

Astrology: Astrology is a way of trying to understand the cycles of nature and our personal relationship with them. Through one's astrological chart, one can look to see what natal health conditions exist and also look at the present and into the future to see what areas of our lives are being affected and potentially how we can head off ill health and promote wellness.

*Atlas Orthogonal: A chiropractic method to evaluate and correct improper alignment based on scientific and biomechanical procedures. Chiropractors can program their instrument to deliver an adjustment without any manipulation at all.

Autogenic Training: A century-old European method for achieving relaxation based upon passive concentration and body awareness of specific sensations. Its effectiveness has been shown in relieving many stress-related disorders including anxiety, tension, insomnia, and examination stress. Persons with chronic medical conditions including migraine, colitis, irritable bowel syndrome, diabetes, high blood pressure, thyroid disease and many other conditions have been shown to benefit from the practice of autogenic training.

Auto-Urine Therapy: This practice comes from Yoga and is the use of one's own urine as food, medicine, restorative, transforming agent and immune system booster. It is sometimes called 'Your Own Doctor'.

Auricular Therapy: A method to relieve pain by stimulating certain points on the ear originally found in ancient Egyptian writings. Many benefits can be achieved by massaging and palpating specific points on the ear.

*Ayurvedic Medicine: Practiced in India for more than 5,000 years, Ayurvedic tradition understands that illness is a state of imbalance among the body's systems that can be detected through such diagnostic procedures as reading the pulse and observing the tongue. Nutrition counselling, massage, natural medications, meditation, and other modalities are used to address a broad spectrum of ailments.

Beck Protocol: The Beck Protocol was developed by Dr. Bob Beck, a physicist, after discovering medical research showing microcurrents disable germs. The program involves the use of three products—a blood cleaner that also makes colloidal silver, a magnetic pulser, and a water ozonator. The protocol is designed to strengthen the immune system and is easily applied at home.

Bach Flower Remedy: These floral remedies are directed at the disharmonies of personality and the emotional state and are mostly aimed at healing emotional conditions rather than physical ones.

Belief Change System: This belief change process uses a combination of different modalities of science, ancient wisdom and Inner Wisdom to transform self-sabotaging beliefs to self-empowering ones at a cellular level and to end false limits and unleash ones greatest potential.

Biofeedback: A method of monitoring minute metabolic changes in one's own body with the aid of sensitive machines. The technique is used especially for stress-related conditions such as asthma, migraines, insomnia, and highblood pressure. Clients learn to make subtle adjustments to move toward a more balanced internal state by consciously visualizing, relaxing, or imagining while observing light, sound, or metered feedback.

BodyTalk: A holistic therapy that allows the body's energy systems to be re-synchronized so they can operate as nature intended. This therapy recognizes that each system, cell, and atom is in constant communication with each other at all times and focuses on reconnecting these lines of communication to enable the body's internal mechanisms to function at optimal levels, thus repairing and preventing disease while rapidly accelerating the healing process. This therapy can be used as a stand-alone system to treat many chronic and acute health problems, or can be integrated with any healthcare regimen to increase its overall effectiveness.

Breath work (Holotropic Breath work): A technique for self-exploration and healing, based on combined insights from modern consciousness research, depth psychology and perennial spiritual practices. The method activates non-ordinary states of consciousness which mobilize the spontaneous healing potential of the psyche. Sustained effective breathing, evocative music, focussed energy work and mandala drawing are components of this subjective journey. 'Holotropic' means 'moving towards wholeness'.

Cellular Therapy: (Also called live cell therapy, cellular suspensions, glandular therapy, fresh cell therapy, siccacell therapy, embryonic cell therapy, and organotherapy) This refers to various procedures in which processed tissue from animal embryos, foetuses or organs, is injected or taken orally. Products are obtained from specific organs or tissues said to correspond with the unhealthy organs or tissues of the recipient.

Chromotherapy or Colour Therapy: The use of colour in the form of coloured light to produce beneficial or healing effects.

Chelation Therapy: A series of intravenous injections of the synthetic amino acid EDTA, designed to detoxify the body. It is also often used to treat arteriosclerosis. Most frequently, this is administered in an osteopathic or medical doctor's office and is said to help with the following conditions: Heart Disease, High Blood Pressure, Macular Degeneration, Arthritis, Diabetes, Chronic Fatigue, Angina, Cholesterol, Leg Pains, Fibromyalgia, Stroke, and any symptoms attributed to heavy metals toxicity (see chapter four for a partial list).

Chinese (Oriental) Medicine: Oriental medical practitioners are trained to use a variety of ancient and modern therapeutic methods including acupuncture, herbal medicine, massage, heat therapy, and nutritional and lifestyle counselling to treat a broad range of illnesses.

*Chiropractic Doctor: A Chiropractic Doctor focuses on the relationship between the body's main structures – the skeleton, the muscles and the nerves – and the patient's health. Chiropractors believe that health can be improved and preserved by making adjustments to these structures, particularly to the spinal column. They do not prescribe drugs or perform surgical procedures, although they do refer patients for these services if they are medically indicated.

Colon (Colonic) Therapy: The therapeutic goals of colon therapy are to balance body chemistry, eliminate waste, and restore proper tissue and organ function. Colon therapy releases toxins, cleans the blood, stimulates the immune system, and aids in restoring the pH balance in the body. It is also said to relieve a wide range of symptoms related to colon dysfunction.

Colonic: A colonic is a colon irrigation, the flushing of the large intestine with sanitized, filtered water under gentle pressure to wash out or detoxify it of stagnated fecal material.

*Counselling/Psychotherapy: This broad category covers a range of practitioners, from career counsellors to psychotherapies who treat depression, stress, addiction, and emotional issues. Formats can vary from individual counselling to group therapy. Some therapists may also incorporate bodywork, ritual, energy healing, and other alternative modalities as part of their practice.

Cupping: A traditional Chinese medical technique which applies suction to diseased parts of the body using ceramic glass or bamboo cups in order to increase the regional circulation and thereby promote healing.

Craniosacral Therapy: This is a manual therapeutic procedure for remedying distortions in the structure and function of the craniosacral mechanism - the brain and spinal cord, the bones of the skull, the sacrum, and interconnected membranes. It is used to treat chronic pain, migraine headaches, and a range of other conditions.

Dance/Movement Therapies: Dance and/or movement therapy uses expressive movement as a therapeutic tool for both personal expression and psychological or emotional healing. Practitioners work with people with physical disabilities, addiction issues, sexual abuse histories, eating disorders, and other concerns.

Dentistry, Holistic: Holistic dentists are licensed dentists who bring an interdisciplinary approach to their practice. They may incorporate such methods as homeopathy, nutrition and acupuncture into their treatment plans. Most holistic dentists emphasize wellness and preventive care while avoiding silver-mercury fillings.

Diatomaceous Earth: Taken as a supplement with water or food, it scrubs intestinal walls and cuts up any parasites present in the digestive tract. Additionally, as it passes the digestive tract, it attracts and absorbs pathogens such as bacteria, viruses, protozoa, and fungi. It also absorbs and removes pesticides, heavy metals, and drug residues. The silica in diatomaceous earth is effective in preventing premature aging, can make age spots fade and also help to repair and maintain lung tissue elasticity. Other benefits include lowering blood pressure and bad cholesterol, relieving sore joints, promoting healthier skin, hair, teeth and gums, and hardening nails.

Ear Candling: Primarily used for wax build-up and related hearing problems, ear candling is also used for ear infections and sinus infections. Treatment involves placing the narrow end of a specially designed hollow candle at the entry of the ear canal, while the opposite end is lit.

Electropathy: A specialised system of therapeutics which involves the use of various forms of electric currents for medicinal purposes.

Far Infrared Sauna: Far Infrared Radiation Sauna heat is used as a heat therapy said to aid in weight loss by speeding up the metabolic process of vital organs and endocrine glands. It is also used for injuries as heat stimulates vasodilatation of peripheral blood vessels, bringing oxygen to joints and extremities, speeding the healing of sprains and strains, relieving pain, and helping injured muscles recover faster.

Fasting: Therapeutic fasting or fasting for health is a purifying and rejuvenating process by which toxic waste matters of the body are eliminated and regeneration of diseased tissues occurs.

Feldenkrais Method: A systematic approach to neuromuscular relearning, the proponents of the method indicate it is suited to healthy people who want to increase the flexibility of their bodies and thinking, people with neurological and movement disorders, and those who want to achieve excellence in the arts, sports, or any endeavour.

Feng Shui: An ancient Chinese practice of arranging the home or work environment to promote health, happiness, and prosperity. Consultants may recommend changes in the surroundings - from color selection to furniture placement - in order to promote a healthy flow of chi, or vital energy.

Flower Essences: A method of alleviating negative emotional states that may contribute to illness or hinder personal growth. Drops of a solution infused with the captured "essence" of a flower are placed under the tongue or in a beverage. The practitioner helps the client choose appropriate essences, focusing on the client's emotional state rather than on a particular physical condition.

Gemstone Therapy: Gemstones, with their powerful energies and profound resonance with the human body, are energy medicine tools like other forms of energy medicine. Using the body's inherent healing force to nourish and heal in multiple ways, each type of gemstone embodies a unique energy that can focus and amplify this healing force and produce specific therapeutic effects. Most gemstones are worn in a necklace.

Heliotherapy: This modality uses the positive effects of the sun and is said to be an effective tool in boosting the body's immune system.

Herbalism: Herbalism uses natural plants or plant-based substances to treat a range of illnesses and to enhance the functioning of the body's systems. Though herbalism is not a licensed professional modality in Western countries, herbs are "prescribed" by a range of practitioners.

*Holistic Medicine: This is a term for a healing philosophy that views a patient as a whole person, not as just a disease or a collection of symptoms. In the course of treatment, holistic medical practitioners may address a client's emotional and spiritual dimensions as well as the nutritional, environmental, and lifestyle factors that may contribute to an illness. Many holistic medical practitioners combine conventional forms of treatment with natural or alternative treatments.

*Homoeopathy: A medical system that uses infinitesimally small doses of natural substances called remedies to stimulate a person's immune and defence systems. Conditions homeopathy addresses include infant and childhood diseases, infections, fatigue, allergies, and chronic illnesses such as arthritis.

Hydrotherapy: The application of water typically in a spa environment for therapeutic purposes. Water may be used at various temperatures, in different modes and in different forms.

Hypnotherapy: A means of bypassing the conscious mind and accessing the subconscious, where memories, repressed emotions, and forgotten events may remain accessible. Hypnosis may facilitate behavioural, emotional, or attitudinal change such as weight loss, or smoking cessation. It is also used to treat phobias, stress, and as an adjunct in the treatment of illness.

*Iridology: A diagnostic system based on the premise that every organ has a corresponding location within the iris of the eye, which can serve as an indicator of the individual organ's health or disease. Iridology is used by naturopaths and other practitioners, particularly when diagnosis achieved through standard methods is unclear.

*Insulin Potentiation Treatment: An alternative Cancer treatment. Proponents say by using insulin in conjunction with chemotherapy drugs, significantly less drugs (about 10-15 % of a standard dose) can be targeted more specifically and more effectively to Cancer cell populations, thus virtually eliminating dose-related side-effects while claiming enhancing antineoplastic effects.

Intramuscular Stimulation (Dry needling): In the treatment of trigger points for persons with myofascial pain syndrome, dry needling is an invasive procedure in which a filiform needle is inserted into the skin and muscle directly at a myofascial trigger point. A myofascial trigger point consists of multiple contraction knots, which are related to producing and the continuance of the pain cycle.

Kinesiology: Kinesiology is the study of the human body during movement. There are many disciplines within Kinesiology including anatomy, biomechanics, exercise physiology, motor control, motor learning, neuromuscular physiology, sports psychology, and philosophy.

*Live Blood Cell Analysis: Live blood analysis can provide information about the state of the immune system, possible vitamin deficiencies, amount of toxicity, pH and mineral imbalance, areas of concern and weaknesses, fungus and yeast. Some claim it can spot Cancer and other degenerative immune system diseases up to two years before they would otherwise be detectable or say they can diagnose lack of oxygen in the blood, low trace minerals, lack of exercise, too much alcohol or yeast, weak kidneys, bladder or spleen.

Lymph Drainage Therapy: A therapy to drain and improve the lymphatic vessels of the body.

Magneto Therapy: The art of healing by applying magnets to the diseased parts of the human body.

Massage (Therapeutic): It involves the practice of manipulating a person's muscles and other soft tissue with the intent of improving a person's well-being or health, and may include, but not be limited to, effleurage, deep tissue, percussion, vibration, and joint movement.

Medicinal Marijuana: Depending on the legal jurisdiction, this is a physician-recommended form of medicine that relieves symptoms and is helpful in the treatment of many diseases.

Naturopathic Medicine: Naturopathic physicians work to restore and support the body's own healing abilities using a variety of modalities including nutrition, herbal medicine, homeopathic medicine, and orient medicine.

Network Chiropractic: This refers to a chiropractor that uses Network Spinal Analysis, a method characterized by the sequential application of a number of gentle, specific adjusting techniques. Care progresses through a series of levels that parallel spinal and quality-of-life changes.

Neural Prolotherapy: A treatment for most injuries and chronic joint, tendon, ligament and muscle pain involving injections with a dextrose or mannitol solution immediately under the skin with a very fine needle.

Ohashiatsu: A system of physical techniques, exercise and meditation used to relieve tension and fatigue and induce a state of harmony and peace. The practitioner first assesses a person's state by feeling the hara, the area below the navel. Then, using continuous and flowing movements, the practitioner presses and stretches the body's energy channels, working in unison with the person's breathing.

ONDAMED Therapy: This physiological treatment uses focused pulsed electromagnetic waves to stimulate improvement of systemic functions such as acute injuries, chronic dysfunctions as well as improving stress tolerance levels. The System complements other treatments such as pharmaceuticals, homeopathic remedies and nutritional supplements.

*Oriental Diagnosis: It is a diagnostic procedure by which the patient's pulse is examined to detect disease according to Traditional Chinese Medicine.

Osteopathic Medicine: Osteopathic physicians provide comprehensive medical care, including preventive medicine, diagnosis, surgery, prescription medications, and hospital referrals. In diagnosis and treatment, they focus on the joints, bones, muscles, and nerves and are specially trained in osteopathic manipulative treatment - using their hands to diagnose, treat, and prevent illness.

Pyramid Healing: Using the exact dimensional properties of the ancient Egyptian pyramids, model pyramids are said to preserve foods, sharpen or maintain the sharpness of razor blades, and improve health.

Physiotherapy (Physical Therapy): This therapy includes identifying and maximizing quality of life and movement potential involving patient diagnosis, treatment/intervention, and prevention and rehabilitation, and encompasses physical, psychological, emotional, and social well being.

*Radiesthesia (Muscle testing): The practice of using the body's own awareness of what is beneficial or harmful to it by the use of dowsing or divining to diagnose disease and select remedies. It is a method of arriving at a diagnosis and treatment for any condition using the human being as the diagnostic instrument.

Radionics: A therapy that has grown up around the ability of the human being to use radiesthesia (muscle testing) together with simple instruments to help in the diagnosis of disease in animals, plants and humans and then to treat this disease at a distance without the presence of the patient.

Reconstructive Therapy/Prolotherapy: This reconstructive therapy uses injections of natural substances such as dextrose, glycerine, and phenol in order to stimulate the growth of connective tissue and this strengthens weak or damaged joints, cartilage, ligaments, and tendons. This therapy is used to treat degenerative arthritis, lower back pain, torn ligaments and cartilage, carpal tunnel syndrome, and other conditions.

*Reflexology: A natural healing art based on the principle that there are reflexes in the feet, hands and ears and their referral areas within zone related areas, which correspond to every part, gland and organ of the body. Through application of pressure on these reflexes without the use of tools, crèmes or lotions (primarily the feet) reflexology relieves tension, improves circulation and helps promote the natural function of the related areas of the body.

*Reiki: The use of light hand placements (or hand placements close to the body) to channel healing energies to the recipient. While practitioners may vary widely in technique and philosophy, Reiki is commonly used to treat emotional and mental distress as well as chronic and acute physical problems, and to assist the recipient in achieving spiritual focus and clarity.

Rolfing: A massage technique using deep manipulation of the fascia (connective tissue) to restore the body's natural alignment, which may have become rigid through injury, emotional trauma, and inefficient movement habits. The process involves ten sessions, each focusing on a different part of the body.

Shiatsu: The most widely known form of acupressure, shiatsu has been used in Japan for more than 1,000 years to treat pain and illness and for general health maintenance. Using a series of techniques, practitioners apply rhythmic finger pressure at specific points on the body in order to stimulate chi, or the vital energy.

Sound Therapy: The use of sound waves to heal.

*Teeth as a diagnostic aid: The tooth site and one or more parts of the body share an energy channel or meridian, as it's called in Traditional Chinese Medicine. A disturbance or disharmony in an organ, tissue or gland etc. can cause a problem at a particular tooth site and vice versa. For more information on these acumeridian relationships do an Internet search on *tooth organ map* or *tooth organ chart*.

Tibetan Medicine: This practice evolved as a synthesis of Tibetan, Chinese, Persian and Ayurvedic medicine. The remedies include indigenous herbs, fruits, flowers, metallic powders and minerals given in tablets, and are said to be effective in treating rheumatism, asthma, gastritis, diabetes and many neurological disorders.

Unani: This involves the use of plants and herbs, and the remedies are known to provide cures for diseases such as sinusitis, leucoderma, rheumatism, jaundice and elephantiasis.

Vitamin Therapy: A complementary therapy of vitamin usage combined with other treatments to address a range of illnesses and to enhance the functioning of the body's systems. This therapy assists the immune system in combating diseases such as Chronic Fatigue Syndrome and HIV/AIDS.

*Western/Contemporary Medicine: A comprehensive system which applies health science, biomedical research, and medical technology to diagnose and treat injury and disease, typically through medication/pharmacologically active agents (drugs) or surgery, but also through therapies as diverse as psychotherapy, external splints and traction, prostheses, biologics, ionizing radiation and others.

Whey Protein Isolate: A dietary supplement that can optimize one's immune system.

Yoga Therapy: The use of yoga to address mental and physical problems while integrating body and mind. Yoga has been used as supplementary therapy for diverse conditions such as Cancer, diabetes, asthma and AIDS, and the scope of medical issues where yoga is used as a complementary therapy continues to grow. One of the main goals of yoga is to improve overall well-being through teaching discipline and self-regulation.

*As stated above, I have added an asterisk to those therapies above that I feel may assist you in getting to the root of your issue.

> **Exercise: Receiving all the Help that You Can Get**
>
> As you prepare to meet your doctor, therapist or healing practitioner, treat the occasion as sacred. Be open to receive Divine Wisdom in the form of inspiration, a nudge, Sign, or something said (Golden-tongued Wisdom). These messages could lead you to something new or provide you with clues to how you can do your part to heal. Anything discussed may represent an important area of change you can make to go beyond your present condition (state of consciousness). So be open, receptive and listen, and even ask what you can do. You may be surprised at what comes out.
>
> Reiki, Chiropractic treatments and Reflexology among others, have helped me tune in to inner nudges and awareness.

The art of healing comes from nature, not from the physician.
Therefore the physician must start from nature, with an open mind.
Philippus Aureolus Paracelsus,
German-Swiss Renaissance Physician and Botanist

Now let's put all these techniques, tools and information together and help you create your own integrated healing approach.

14

Every Illness Has a Spiritual Solution

When we are no longer able to change a situation, we are challenged to change ourselves.

Viktor Frankl, Austrian Psychiatrist and Psychotherapist

Grace's Life-transformation

Grace has a dual career as a natural health practitioner and another work assignment that involves a lot of travel. As she was about to board a flight one day, an airline staff person approached her to let her know she needed to call her family on an urgent matter. Upon talking to her brother-in-law, she heard that her mother had just died of a massive heart attack. She was in total shock. Her life was loaded up with stress as she had just purchased her first home after many years of renting, and she had yet to close on the deal. Her loss just added other burdens, having to look after the funeral arrangements as well as pack up a quarter lifetime of possessions and move. "The move was hard," she told me, "letting go of the old apartment and its memories."

Thirty days later she started to lose weight, rapidly dropping from one-hundred-and-five to eighty-eight pounds over a three week period. But she continued to work. A few more weeks down the road she started to get comments from co-workers about how gaunt she looked, yet she still resisted seeing a doctor. Finally after six months of denial about her condition, she relented and scheduled a visit. It wasn't good. Her doctor thought she might have thyroid Cancer! He referred her on to an Endocrinologist who diagnosed her condition as Graves' disease. "There is a lot of mystery surrounding this condition as to causes and cures," he informed her, but he gave her some literature to read. The information indicated that one of the triggers for Graves' is psychological and emotional stress.

Facing Unresolved Issues

"I remember reflecting on my life at that time," Grace told me. "I realized I had not told my mother about my new condo, wanting to surprise her when I closed the deal. It felt like an unresolved issue. I had never settled down and married, had children, bought a home and become a doctor like they had hoped. I realized deep down I wanted to please my mother with this big step of settling down, but now I could not share my joy with her. I could see subconsciously I had been always trying to please my parents.

"My condition had caused my dramatic weight loss because I could not keep food down. Diarrhea was also a big part of the issue, plus I had tremors in my hands as well as heart palpitations. With all of this, my anxiety soared. The Graves' was speeding things up and I was constantly hot. I was told the condition could lead to a heart attack, but I was not paying attention, I was in denial.

"On accepting treatment, the doctor's protocol to control my metabolism involved some horrible medicine which gave me hives and skin rashes. However it worked, allowing me to regain my weight and to stop shaking. The specialist though, also wanted to give me radiation treatments to prevent Cancer from developing. But I knew it would destroy my thyroid, an important gland that controls metabolism, affecting every function of the body. I'd need to be placed on synthetic hormones for the rest of my life. I steadfastly declined the radiation, but accepted the prescription cortisone cream for the terrible skin conditions caused by the drugs.

Taking Responsibility Physically and Spiritually

"At this point in my experience I realized deep down I needed to take responsibility for my condition. I went for acupuncture and also saw a Chinese Medicine specialist who gave me some traditional Chinese herbal remedies. Moving more into the process of taking responsibility for what I was experiencing, I began to use all the spiritual responses I could muster to engage all my senses. What emerged was emotional – shock and a sense of guilt. I realized I felt like a failure not fulfilling my parent's dream. I had many talents as a child and youth including high academic aptitudes, skilled piano playing and creative writing. My parents had high expectations, yet I knew I had a different calling other than getting married, having kids and developing my current talents. But my parents being Asian held these strong traditional expectations.

"I had reinvigorated my contemplation practice and had begun to use creative visualization. One day, looking for techniques to help me heal, I read a book on spiritual guides and inner world temples, and as I scanned down a list of these inner masters, I saw the name Ori Diogo. I read his noted role: He was in charge of healing on the Astral (emotional) Plane, and his name immediately resonated with me. In my daily contemplation/spiritual exercise I began to sing his name out loud and picture myself in the spiritual healing temple working with him in the higher worlds. I'd see myself on a table singing HU, envisaging the colour orange around my throat. I could feel it and see it. I also enveloped myself in a blue light to heal my emotions.

"As time went on, I went from initially pleading and bargaining (with the thought of Cancer gripping me), asking for this condition to be taken away, to accepting things for what they were - to a state of peacefulness. I was letting go and in that process I shifted and felt lifted. My contemplations and visualization exercises were now giving me gentle reassurances from the Holy Spirit. I got a strong feeling it would all work out as I let go of self-judgement.

Self-discovery Exercises

"Part of my self-discovery process involved using my writing talents. I kept a healing journal, tracking my feelings and emotions – I got it all out. For me it was a way of getting rid of it. What also helped me was an exercise, writing a special phrase fifteen times: 'I am loved.' I would express it in stanzas like a poem, a mantra. Through writing I realized I had not been expressing myself or speaking my truth! A deep seated fear of ridicule was coming from my Asian cultural background, and being female. I discovered part of my healing was learning to speak up.

"Today, I'm in remission. On my last visit to the doctor I was jumping for joy when he told me I would no longer need the drugs. However, I continue to take Chinese herbs to keep in balance and I have acupuncture treatments regularly.

"I'm continuing to find my voice and this is even finding its way into public presentations I'm doing. I'm now much more relaxed about this. I'm listening and paying attention to inner nudges. Before, I was an overachiever, addicted to perfection, so always controlled by fear of criticism. Today, I'm much more relaxed.

Healing Happens on All Levels

"I finally came to understand that healing happens on all levels. I reached an acceptance of myself the way I am. What I really needed was self-acceptance. And I needed to experience this on a cellular level, not being attached to any particular outcome. I experienced a lot of growth at that time, accepting myself in my own skin. Growing up being female and Asian, a visible minority with a sensitive constitution in a Western society, I had even chosen a career involving a lot of travel and this underscored my issue of not seeming to make a commitment to being here. My parents wanted me to be a doctor but I became a holistic practitioner instead. But I burned out of that career because I would go go go. I seemed to be a Type A personality, always trying to please my clients at my own expense. I wasn't honoring myself."

When I asked Grace if her dreams had provided her with any guidance or insights, she recalled one in particular that was a turning point in her healing journey. "I was taking a walk with my spiritual guide in the dream," she reflected. "He was asking: 'Do you understand? Do you understand?' As time went on I had to learn where this issue was coming from. It came back to accepting myself the way I am – self love. I was paying lip service to the idea up until that point. It just wasn't sinking in. Through this illness experience, it has now sunk in!"

Grace continued, "Graves' Disease turned out to be a big life-transformation for me. My healing even translated into new awakenings about my relationships – that I was addicted to dysfunctional liaisons. I realized I had chosen partners who were emotionally unavailable, and this was detrimental to my spiritual growth. Today, I'm totally free. I no longer choose involvements out of need. If I choose to be with a partner, they will also be on a spiritual journey too.

Healing: It Comes Back to Love

"I can also see I've modified so that I'm not so hard on myself. I'm perfect by not being perfect. I'm accepting each moment as perfect. I'm now more authentic, yet when I speak up, it is with grace. I've now accepted as fact that I'm loved by my parents and God. I'm letting something come in instead of blocking it. This something is love. I now have an expanded awareness of it. It is love that we're here for. It all comes back to loving yourself first, then loving God, family and others."

Grace shared her final thoughts on healing for others: "Always remember to come back to love. It's so simple yet so profound.

Giving service is part of this love. We are here to serve others. If you embrace this in your whole being, healing can occur."

∼

Healing Requires Change

Viktor Frankl's quote at the beginning of this chapter reminds me of the expression, if you change nothing, nothing will change. The main theme of this book is change; healing requires a willingness on your part to make changes in your life. Our comfort zones can be very subtle, unnoticeable much of the time. So part of our discovery process is looking at ourselves honestly. This is where contemplation/meditation can be such a great asset helping you to bypass the mental patterns that you have established over the years. Also seeing the Signs and messages around you can help you get to the heart, to see what needs to shift.

Spiritual Protection in Avoiding a Health Issue

One day I was particularly attracted to an article on Facebook a friend had posted. It was on EMR's (electromagnetic radiation) and went into depth on issues and dangers I hadn't seen before. I had been given a new wireless router and tablet and my computer was now routed through this device resulting in wireless signals running all the time in our house. A few months earlier, I had some heightened EMR concerns after this issue was also mentioned at a spiritual seminar I attended and had decided to turn my cell phone off most of the time, but I had not made any changes with other devices. However one night before bed I had asked Spirit for a dream that could help me in my outer life, and woke up with this seemingly bland dream in my head. However as I wrote it down, it dawned on me how important this message was. In the dream I was riding as a passenger in a powerful electric car. An old friend was driving the car and was running through stoplights on the yellow signals – not through the red lights but almost. He was pushing it. On checking my dream dictionary which I record at the back of my spiritual journal, I remembered that a car seen in my dreams is my symbol for Soul, my vehicle, and this car was electric and very powerful. The dream was telling me I was living in this very powerful electrical field and the yellow lights were a cautionary symbol. The friend was an old friend and to me symbolized an older consciousness. The dream combined with the Facebook article, a Sign, was enough to move me to fix the router connection so I could run my computer hard-wired to the Internet and switch on the Wi-Fi router only when needed for the tablet.

I am grateful for this protection I received from Spirit, possibly avoiding future illness due to a compromised immune system or other issues, yet to be discovered.

Something Needs to Change

In putting this process of healing into motion, something needs to change, or some things need to change. The latter can be more probable from my experience. So your blueprint is before you. The first action is to accept that change is necessary. Remember, a healing is a change in consciousness, and a change in consciousness involves a change in beliefs and a new level of faith in the Creator and in yourself.

Discovering what needs to shift is the journey. What options or emotional responses to others can you put on the table? How much of your life, the way you go about your life, is open for alteration?

This change that you undertake will in all likelihood change you in ways you had not expected or anticipated. Are you ready for a new you? What is your well-being worth? Is it worth a job, a relationship, giving up assets or things? These are tough questions, but once you are able to let go of certain attachments, discovering the causes and making shifts can be much easier. You may not have to let go of money for example, but by being willing to do so, (for example, letting go of the need for a certain amount of money) opens up new possibilities. This letting go brings us back to the greatest teacher – pain – whether it is physical, emotional or mental. Sooner or later we will move forward into healing and into freedom by accepting change and letting go.

Once you accept an injury or an illness as something that can benefit you, e.g. strengthen you in an area of your life where you have felt weak, incompetent, or anxious before, you will start connecting with it. This connection with the "problem" then allows your energy and emotion to flow into it and release the emotional barriers to spontaneous healing.

Andreas Moritz, author of Cancer is Not a Disease, It's a Survival Mechanism

At this point we are acknowledging change must occur. Now we want to envisage what levels of change we can bring about.

Exercises in Uncovering Disharmonies

Now that you can accept that you can let go in various areas of your life, you can begin your search for the root areas of change. The rest of this chapter offers a number of ways you can dig a little deeper and uncover some disharmonies in your life.

Exercise: Your Physical Body

Start on the physical level. Take a day to contemplate on your physical surroundings including home life, work life, friends, family, and other activities. Which areas bring you joy, satisfaction or harmony?

Which areas make you feel tense, hurt, uncomfortable or anxious?

Honest answers to these questions may lead to areas that need rebalancing.

Exercise: Facilitating Change:

Change something about your daily routine. Choose a different route to work. Sit somewhere different on the bus, at your breakfast table or watching TV. Change the order of your morning routine in getting ready for your day. What can you change today?

This exercise will open you up to new points-of-view. It will break up old patterns and habits and bring about a new openness and receptivity to change.

Exercise: Reviewing Your Emotional Body

Next, review your emotions.

Emotions such as feeling blue, depression, self-pity, suspicion, lying, fear, annoyance, boredom, mistrust and jealously can be very destructive to your well-being. Society, though, can often condone these emotions and make you feel that these are OK to express. (We like to give these issues disease names so that we can accept them.) You need to get out of this trap! Remember, what others can do is not what you can do. Some people can smoke, drink, swear and express anger until they are 104. We are all wired differently. So it is important to be aware that these negative emotions are harmful and can be disease-causing if indulged in for longer periods of time.

How often are you upset, irritated, feeling stressed?

Do you feel resistant, fearful, depressed or down?

When do these feelings occur?

Again, these answers provide more clues to what is happening to you and to how you perceive things are unfolding in your life.

There are two sides to the coin though: First, how can you move closer to the positive pole? What changes can you make to accomplish this?

Second, what feelings, emotions or predilections can you let go of that are no longer serving you?

Exercise: Changing Your Future - Your Causal Body

How can you change today so that your tomorrows will be better? This is really about leading a life with less karma, setting less karma in motion.

Review the chapter on karma. How can you be more loving, accepting, respectful, joyful etc.?

How can you change your future by changing who you are and how you respond to people today? Like attracts like. If you want calmness, you need to be a force for calm. If you want respect, give respect. If you want to receive love, you need to give love to others. It's that simple, but can be difficult at the same time.

From the list of spiritual qualities in the appendix at the back of the book select five qualities you want to have more of in your life.

The next step is to make a collage. Cut five images from a magazine that represent each of the five qualities and paste them on a sheet of paper and label them if you wish. Now post this up somewhere where you can see it every day.

By placing your attention on these positive qualities you will begin to change your life by attracting people, situations and activities into your life that are a reflection of these qualities.

Exercise: For Your Mind Body

Now you need to examine your thought patterns. Go back and re-read chapter ten on thoughts, beliefs and attitudes. Take a day or longer to note the areas where you feel you could do better. The key here is to uncover the basic ideas, beliefs and, thoughts you identify with.

What beliefs are attractive to you and what beliefs do you strongly reject? In other words, do you hold strongly held beliefs one way or the other?

These areas represent healing opportunities that can lead to creating a new level of harmony within you. This is because you are trying to reach a state of balance and being too much one way or the other, for or against anything, can be causing imbalances at other levels of your being.

Thoughts are things. They reflect back to you. What you think, you become.

Ask yourself, What am I becoming?

Exercise: Uncovering Dominant Thoughts

What are your dominant thoughts?

Beside each word, write three descriptive words that immediately come to mind.

Work

Home

Family

Hobbies and Sports

Health

Finances

Entertainment

Wait a few hours or a day and then review your descriptive words and underline those in each area that represent a state of becoming that is moving in the wrong direction for you.

Integrating Your Purification

Exercise: Total Integration

Write one physical step you can take to change your life.

Write one emotional change you can make to change how you relate to others.

Write one thought, belief or attitude you can modify or reverse.

Setting Your Goal(s) from a Spiritual Perspective

Exercise: Creating a New Consciousness of Well-being

Assuming total well-being is your goal, answer the following questions with the future in mind.

What physical qualities are present in my life when I have reached my goal? (Can you can walk, run, ski, bicycle, travel, sleep soundly, feel joy, laugh often etc?)

How do I **feel** when I have reached my goal? For thought-starters, see the list of spiritual qualities in the appendix at the back of this book and write down a few.

How do I make others feel when I am around them? Am I an uplifting person or a downer?

How have my thoughts, beliefs, or attitudes changed when I have reached my goal? Are you more open, reflective vs. reactive, supportive, a better listener, willing to let others have their opinions without strong opposition?

You have now created a set of expectations about your future in terms of the qualities you wish to have in your life when you have met your goals. You have set your goals from a spiritual perspective.

A true spiritual healing first heals the spiritual condition that caused the symptoms to appear in the physical body.

Harold Klemp, Author of *Spiritual Wisdom on Health and Healing*

It Really Comes Down to a Willingness to Change

The main theme of this book has been change – and when you are open in this way, new realizations about yourself can flood in, healing at all levels. Let's reflect back on the people featured in this book and what their journeys revealed. As you read these summaries, think about what each can teach you about yourself.

Diane's contemplations led to acceptance, and surrender to Spirit opened her receptivity to knee surgery, overcoming her fears in the process. Her journaling speeded her recovery and she discovered that all the answers to all our challenges are given to us if we ask. She says, "Love what you are given. Love the gifts of life."

Ian's stroke was a life-altering event for him, but decoding significant dreams helped him with acceptance of his new limitations. His daily contemplations have greatly assisted him with his spiritual growth; he has gained a better understanding of detachment and compassion which have been his key awakenings.

Ted, Oliver's personal training client discovered the healing power of the HU as he overcame treatment pain and subsequently opened up to his spiritual side. Oliver is feeling the joy of helping others on several dimensions, confidently sharing his spirituality in his work.

Dustin's severe burns and his two-year healing process propelled him into a spiritual awakening beginning at age 14 and a realization of his true mission in life – helping others heal.

Facing M.S., Roger has made many new spiritual discoveries about himself, but chiefly that he is here to reach a higher state of love which embodies for him patience and tolerance. He is constantly working in contemplation with his spiritual guide, asking for direction as new symptoms appear. He has learned to be clear about his questions so that his answers are clear as well.

Following the loss of his wife to Cancer, Timothy's daily contemplations kept his heart open to Spirit, assisting him in moving through his grief. He has also let go of a lot of anger in the process and is more authentic – being more himself and discarding fears along the way.

Caroline fully surrendered her sciatic pain to Spirit after suffering for two years and this new letting go opened her to help from others. She uncovered deep-seated anger and quickly healed through exercises in forgiveness.

In her later years, Anastasia was able to see the karma in her life-long "rotten back" but she has also discovered through a series of dreams how several relationships in her life needed to be healed, revealing in the process attitudes and emotions that needed to be purified within her.

Limiting beliefs holding her career back were made visible to Veronica through chronic neck pain. As part of her healing process, she uncovered how her behaviors in a past life are part of her challenges today and how these have subtly shaped her beliefs and fears.

Heavy metals poisoning moved Bonnie into a healing quest and created a connection with an intuitive healer. His provocative suggestion opened her up to a need to recognize and resolve outmoded beliefs about her self-worth, buried within hidden fears.

Candice's brain firestorm was the catalyst she finally needed to completely eliminate sugar from her life. More recently her departure from gluten has led to major inner changes. She tells us: "The healing process has made me realize how I need to purify myself on all levels, and to do this to be the most benefit to my planet, my world. I ask myself, 'How can I be better, more kind, more loving?'"

Eleven operations later, Jill is back together again after her airplane crash, but is not the same person. Her healing odyssey involved wave upon wave of realizations about what emotions and thought patterns needed to be purified within her, moving her into a greater spiritual consciousness of being.

Rebecca's world was turned upside down with the death and betrayal she experienced, but her transition into a new life, finding her spiritual path, awaited her after taking responsibility for her past actions and finding a new ability to express her feelings freely.

Amanda's journey with skin Cancer led her to a greater respect for the choices others make. Following her dreams and journaling her inner and outer experiences and with a strong connection with her inner guide, she found the new modality that provided a lasting healing. At the same time she replaced fears with a deeper understanding of love, unearthing buried grief as part of her healing process.

In facing Graves' disease with the help of her contemplations, Grace learned that healing happens on all levels. Self-acceptance was her key – as she told me, "being perfect by not being perfect." Overall she found an expanded awareness of love.

Keys to Success

These shared experiences embody the process of spiritual healing that each found in their own way and in their own time. Each needed to uncover something new, something uniquely their own in order to heal on all levels. Taking action brought unfoldment to each as they did what they could to bring to light the message(s) hidden in their challenges. Here is what proved successful:

Having a regular spiritual practice such as contemplation, meditation and yoga;

Enhancing their connection with Spirit by singing or chanting HU or other spiritually charged word-sounds;

Journaling their inner and outer experiences, making it easier to see patterns, connections and answers;

Asking for help in solving their challenge (not to ask for their challenge to be solved).

Following signs, messages and information that are placed in one's path. Some describe this as following a cookie crumb trail, one thing leading to the next, and;

Surrendering to Spirit (God), letting go and opening up to new possibilities.

There is Always One More Step in the Journey of Soul!

I invite you to move forward on your journey, be open to change, expect the unexpected and prepare to discover new things about yourself by taking action, working with these tools. In the process you too can uncover the hidden root causes of your illness, injury or disease.

Appendix

Spiritual Qualities for Health and Harmony

Honesty, Forgiveness, Humor, Loving, Detachment, Contentment, Humility, Joy, Enthusiasm, Sharing, Respect, Flexibility, Trust, Harmony, Listening, Caring, Empathy, Grace, Charity, Discipline, Order, Purity, Kindness, Freedom, Openness, Truthfulness, Nurturing, Loyalty, Ingenuity, Discretion, Effectiveness, Reliability, Resourcefulness, Service, Clarity, Prosperity, Commitment, Punctuality, Neatness, Excellence, Optimism, Accuracy, Achievement, Originality, Admiration, Organization, Advancement, Persistence, Personal Growth, Appreciation, Frankness, Friendship, Education, Efficiency, Encouragement, Mastery, Fun, Volunteerism, Cooperation, Acceptance, Gratitude, Thankfulness, Openness, Helpfulness, Cheerfulness, Responsibility, Serenity, Communication, Inspiration, Abundance, Beauty, Play, Compassion, Strength, Surrender, Tenderness, Adventure, Faith, Peace, Balance, Patience, Flexibility, Transformation, Courage, Release, Spontaneity, Integrity, Willingness, Healing, Right Discrimination (making right choices), Simplicity, Purpose, Synthesis, Confident, Enthusiastic, Faithful, Happy, Positive, Sincerity, Tolerant, Understanding, Courage, Supportive, Giving, Hopeful

These qualities are aspects of love!

Made in the USA
Charleston, SC
22 September 2014